Meditation

A Key to New Horizons in God

E. Bernard Jordan

ISBN 0-939241-11-0

Meditation: Key to New Horizons in God

2nd Printing

MEDITATION--THE KEY TO UNLOCK NEW HORIZONS IN GOD is dedicated to one of my most treasured mentors, Prophetess Loretta Taylor, who has impacted the lives of my family and Zoe Ministries with her Godly wisdom, fervent prayers, and prophetic insight.

In Gratitude

We'd like to give the following individuals a special thank you for their faithfulness and support in helping to make our dream come true:

Pastor James & Sandra Lilly &
Eagles Summit Christian
Fellowship Church
Janice Miles
Carleen McDowell
Paul McFarlane
Sandra McGill
Pastor Connie Miles
Kimberly Monk
Pamela & Magolia Moore
Pamela Murray
Earlene B. Oganitmein
Marilyn Oliver &
Jennifer Fontus
Elizabeth Phillips
George & Elaine Reid
Amanda Sears
Rev. Michael Smith
Joy Y. Stevenson
Pastor & Mrs. Samuel Walston Jr.
Linda W. Washington
Prophetess Barbara Webster
Willie J. Wesby

Brenda Anderson
Nichelle Austin
Gloria Bracey
Alfred & Ann Briscoe
Cynthia L. Clarke
Bishop Vincent D. &
Mariea Claxton
LaVelle Cook
Sandra Cooper
Mother Shirley Culpepper
Elise DaCruz
Pastor William & Jane Darrisaw
Karen L. Davis
Pastor Richard Eberiga
Minister William & Andrea Floyd
Cleo Ford
Buck & Catanna Gibson
Raymond Godley
Ezra & Betsie Green
Cecilia Henderson
Melanie Johnson
Minister Olivia Johnson
Debra A. Jordan
Elder Fitzgerald King

Because of their generosity and obedience to the Spirit of God, we know that they have opened the door for miracles, and we believe that He shall cause the gems of wisdom that are contained within these pages to be made manifest in each of their lives, for the reward of the Lord is sure and addeth no sorrow!

In His Love and Service,
Bishop E. Bernard & Pastor Debra Jordan

TABLE OF CONTENTS

AUTHOR'S PREFACE

Our lives are filled with a continuous litany of thoughts and images that are assimilated by our minds as truth or fallacy. In our relationship with God, it is He Who seeks to reveal unto us the essence of His reality and the fullness of His glory. Meditation is the avenue which we must take to allow our finite minds to begin to approach and digest the Infinity of God.

The Scriptures, which are the revelation of God unto us, possess the inherent power to effect transformation in our lives; thus thrusting us towards being changed from glory to glory so that we may reflect the image of Christ Jesus in our world. Because of the soulish and negative impact of images that have bombarded our lives, it is imperative that we begin to allow ourselves to be "brainwashed"---to wash our minds free of pessimism, religiosity, and traditionalism--so that we can be free to attain to the high calling and quality of life that has been promised to us through Jesus Christ.

It is in the milieu of meditation--those quiet times when only that which is of God is thought upon--that metamorphosis takes place.

MEDITATION--THE KEY TO NEW HORIZONS IN GOD has been written as a clarion call to restore the lost art of meditation back into its rightful place within the Body of Christ. New Age and eastern religions have taken that which was part of the heritage of the Believer and brought it into a devilish display of soulish power. These are the days that God desires to display His truth in the midst of the enemy's chicanery, for they that hunger and thirst after righteousness shall truly be filled by Him.

CHAPTER 1
The Need To Be Transformed

I beseech you therefore, brethren, by the mercies of God, that ye present your bodies a living sacrifice, holy, acceptable unto God, which is your reasonable service.

And be not conformed to this world: but be ye transformed by the renewing of your mind, that ye may prove what is that good, and acceptable, and perfect, will of God.

(Romans 12: 1,2)

The Word of God will transform you. It will change you into a positive, victorious person. It will release the power of God in your life, taking you from one

1

level of glory to another. It will transform you into the image of God.

> "And all of us, as with unveiled face, [because we] continue to behold [in the Word of God] as in a mirror the glory of the Lord, are constantly being transfigured into His very own image in ever increasing splendor and from one degree of glory to another; [for this comes] from the Lord [Who is] the Holy Spirit."

(II Corinthians 3:18, AMP).

Transfiguration and transformation takes place only one way: by meditating on the Word of God. Consequently, many people come to know Jesus Christ as Savior, but without the art of meditation, they never go through a period of transformation. The Word of God is the vehicle that saves us, keeps us, and has the ability to transform us.

Jesus took three of His disciples to the Mount of Transfiguration (or the Mount of Transformation). Peter, James, and John saw Jesus transfigured. "...and his face did shine as the sun, and his raiment was white as the light" (Matthew 17:2).

God wants to bring about this same transformation in our lives. He wants to transform our thinking. He wants to change the way we walk, but these changes must begin in our thought life. Meditation is the mountain or foundation upon which our transformation will take place.

2

Freedom From Negative Traditions

Just as Jesus was transfigured, we are to be transfigured (or renewed) in our minds. "Renewing" means a constant or continual renovation, which makes a person different from the way they were in the past. That is why in the process of renewing the mind, a deprogramming must take place before a reprogramming can transpire.

There are some things that must be dethroned that have been programmed into our minds. For instance, a mother who has had a bad marriage may tell her daughter, "All men are no good." The daughter gets married, but if her mind is not renewed by meditating on the Word of God, in the back of her mind will be the message, *"All men are no good."*

Another negative tradition concerning marriage is: "You need to keep something on the side for a rainy day, because you never know when your husband is going to leave you." The person with the unrenewed mind starts saving, making preparations for the day when the husband will leave. By carrying such a negative belief, you will enter into a relationship based upon distrust. Marriage is a covenant relationship. There is no such thing as a prenuptial agreement in the Kingdom of God. Covenant is exchanging with one another - all that I have belongs to you, and everything that you have now belongs to me; we belong to each other.

When the woman keeps a nest egg on the side, she is never able to give herself totally to her husband. She is never able to look to him as the man he's supposed to be.

Many mindsets have been handed down from one generation to the next. Things your parents, grandparents, or great grandparents have told you. I'd like to address some of those "sacred idols" we have accepted from an early age. A very popular (familiar) one is expressed in a song we used to sing:

Give me that old time religion,

Give me that old time religion,

Give me that old time religion,

It's good enough for me.

It was good for my mother,

It was good for my mother,

It was good for my mother,

It's good enough for me.

It was good for my father,

It was good for my father,

It was good for my father,

It's good enough for me.

We need a revelation of Gospel truth! That which was good enough for our mothers and fathers in their day, is not necessarily sufficient for us today. We need to move into present day truth. For example, we cannot do what Noah did in his day. The Bible says Noah was perfect. He built an ark as God directed him. If we were to build an ark today, we would be out of the order and flow of the Holy Spirit for the time and day in which we live.

When your parents or grandparents were growing up, the spiritually "in" thing to do was to get filled with the Holy Ghost and speak in tongues. God is still doing this, but He is also bringing us into revelation that is pertinent to the world we live in today.

In the time of Martin Luther, people received salvation by faith. That was the "in" thing of that hour. Some people pitched their tents and camped during that move of God, refusing to shift to the present move of God. They have not pulled up their stakes. They are still worshipping on yesterday's manna, not receiving the fresh manna (or Word of the Lord) for today.

The songs we sing set the pace for our victory or defeat. They are programming our minds. We are to sing the Word.

Colossians 3:16 says, *"Let the word of Christ dwell in you richly in all wisdom; teaching and admonishing one another in psalms and hymns and spiritual songs, singing with grace in your hearts to the Lord."*

We are to be taught and admonished through psalms and hymns and spiritual songs. The Church becomes what it sings. Singing can be almost

5

hypnotic. It is able to bypass the intellect and get down into your spirit man. Singing has a way of programming the listener. People who attend church can eagerly proclaim,

"Man, have you heard we are going to fly away?"

"Yes!" Where did they get that? Not from reading it in Scripture, but by hearing it in a song.

There is another group of people who are always saying, "I'm climbing up on the rough side of the mountain." That is contrary to the Scriptures! The Word of God does not speak of climbing mountains! Jesus said, "...*say unto this mountain, be thou removed..!*" He didn't tell you to climb it!

The church has been habitually singing from the realm of her experience rather than the standpoint of truth.

We are taught and admonished by what we sing. I remember a church song from years ago:

"Nobody knows the troubles I've seen,

Nobody knows but Jesus.

Nobody knows the troubles I've seen,

Glory Hallelujah!

Sometimes I'm up,

Sometimes I'm down,

Oh, yes, Lord! Sometimes I'm level to the ground!

Oh, yes, Lord"!

Looking at the words of this song, one does not have to wonder why victory doesn't manifest in the lives of people who sing it! To renew our minds, we need to sing songs of triumph. We must cease from being churches with a survival mentality, and become churches of a kingdom mentality, that are here to take over until Jesus comes!

When Paul addressed the Romans in Romans 12:1,2 he said, *"I beseech you therefore, brethren, by the mercies of God, that ye present your bodies a living sacrifice, holy, acceptable unto God, which is your reasonable service. And be not conformed to this world: but be ye transformed by the renewing of your mind, that ye may prove what is that good, and acceptable, and perfect, will of God."*

At times I have asked myself the question, "Who is the biggest giver in all the world?" I then see that God, as a result of His giving, has parted with more than anyone else. He lost one of His best angels, Lucifer, who took a third of the angels (God's heavenly host) with him. God created the earth and gave the rule of it to man, who fell from his place of rule. This left man ruled in an unregenerated state while under the prince of the power of the air (Satan). What does God do to rectify this situation? Give again! He gave His only Son, Jesus, so He could regain many sons. Jesus said on one occasion, *"In my Father's house are many mansions: if it were not so, I would have told you. I go to prepare a place for you..."* (John 14:2).

(We read this at every funeral)! We get excited about this: "My mansion in the sky! Lord, I'm sending up timber." The Bible says that everything that is wood, hay, and stubble, will be burned up!

One translation says, "In my Father's house are many dwelling places. If it were not so, I would have told you...I go away to prepare a place for you..."

Jesus has already gone away and prepared a place for us. As His children, we are even now seated with Him in heavenly places.

> *"But God, who is rich in mercy, for his great love wherewith he loved us, Even when we were dead in sins, hath quickened us together with Christ, (by grace ye are saved;) And hath raised us up together, and made us sit together in heavenly places in Christ Jesus:"*

(Ephesians 2:4-6).

Jesus has already prepared a place for us. He is saying, "I want you to abide in the now." That is why Paul could say:

> *"Let us therefore come boldly unto the throne of grace, that we may obtain mercy, and find grace to help in time of need."*

(Hebrews 4:16).

The traditional pie-in-the-sky type thinking keeps us from entering into the present dwelling place that the Lord has prepared for us.

We must walk in present day revelation, not the revelation of our parents or grandparents. We cannot sit down and camp at the fire of the 1906 Azusa Street revival. We must move on. God is saying something greater. Each generation brings a revelation to the earth, therefore, we are to walk in it.

The Lord spoke to me, in a prophetic word, that this next generation He is raising up will be a generation of provokers. In December 1989, He said it is a generation that will not compromise. This is a generation that will not compromise. This is a generation that will not "sit" and hold down the fort, but they will storm the gates of hell to fulfill the purposes of God.

Many people have come to the saving knowledge of Jesus, but have never become established in the Word, or allowed the Word to become a part of them.

The Bible says,

> *"And the Word was made flesh, and dwelt among us, (and we beheld his glory, the glory as of the only begotten of the Father,) full of grace and truth"*

> (John 1:14).

God wants us to become His Word made visible to mankind. The transformation must come, but it will come only through the renewing of the mind.

Romans 12:2 says, *"And be not conformed to this world..."* This means, "do not be fashioned after the order of this world." This world is not to be the trendsetter. The Church is to be the trendsetter.

The Church does not have to go to the stages and theatres of the world to get an understanding of choreography. Dance is a form of worship unto God. God is to be praised and worshipped. The Psalmist says,

> "...let the children of Zion be joyful in their King: let them praise his name in the dance: let them sing praises unto him with the timbrel and harp. For the Lord taketh pleasure in his people: ..."

(Psalm 149:2-4).

All forms of art are to be used to worship God and to bring glory and honor to the King of kings and the Lord of lords. We are not to be fashioned after the order of the world, but we are to be transformed. The only way to be transformed is "... by the renewing of your mind..." (Romans 12:2).

There are two different Greek words for "world" : "aion" which means "age"; and "kosmos", which means "order or arrangement of things." (The word cosmetic comes from kosmos). When you are putting on cosmetics, you are arranging your face. There is nothing wrong with cosmetics. Some people *need* arrangement!

Let's find out how to be changed by examining some things about transformation. The renewing of the mind means "to make new." If we, as believers, are willing, our moral and spiritual vision can be changed to become as God's. The Greek word for renewal is "ANAKAINOSIS".

The process of transformation takes place through the vehicle called renewal. Our minds must be renewed, for the mind is the seat of our reflections or the area where we have the ability to play back or imagine. If you meditate upon your failures, or ponder on negative things of the past, you will not obtain the victory.

> *Finally, brethren, whatsoever things are true, whatsoever things are honest, whatsoever things are just, whatsoever things are pure, whatsoever things are lovely, whatsoever things are of good report; if there be any virtue, and if there be any praise, think on these things.*

(Philippians 4:8)

David began to replay his victories in his mind and was able to slay a giant. When no man would take the challenge of the champion Goliath and fight for the cause of Israel, David said to Saul, "...*Let no man's heart fail because of him; thy servant will go and fight with this Philistine*" (I Samuel 17:32).

When Saul said to David he was just a youth and not able to go and fight against this Philistine, David knew his God and began to play back in his mind the victories God had given him. He said, *"Thy servant*

11

slew both the lion and the bear: and this uncircumcised Philistine (one that did not know God) shall be as one of them, seeing he hath defied the armies of the living God." (I Samuel 17:36).

Some people entertain thoughts such as: "When I was out in the world, I was on drugs." Now, that is the truth, but it is not a good report nor is it pure, so you shouldn't be thinking about it.

Others lie when they testify, "Thank God for saving me from a miserable life of sin." You weren't miserable in sin! The Bible says sin is pleasurable for a season. The Scripture says Moses chose *"...rather to suffer affliction with the people of God than to enjoy the pleasures of sin for a season"* (Hebrews 11:25).

This is why we do not encourage people to testify about when they were in sin, because the Bible says to think on the things that are true, pure, and of a good report. This may have been true, but it is not a good report. There is nothing pure in it. Therefore, you do not have any business dwelling on it. You are a new person in Christ, old things have passed away, and all things have become new.

Notice that God does not make all new things, but He causes all things to become new. When you come to the altar, He is not going to remove your mind and say, "Let me put a brand new mind in you." It just doesn't work that way.

As you sit under the Word of God and meditate upon the Word, your thoughts and ideas are being changed as your mind is being renewed, and you are being trained to think in line with God's Word.

Arousing an Appetite for the Word

In raising children, many parents try to awaken their child's appetite for nutritious food. They touch the child's palate with food in an attempt to awaken a taste for it. In the same way, the renewal of the mind can come forth only as we awaken our appetites to the Word of God.

The palate is the roof of the mouth. It is a place where the tastebuds can be awakened. What a parent would do to a baby is chew the food for them, then proceed to place it in the baby's mouth. By doing this, the parent causes the child's appetite to awaken to table food.

In the same way, a person's appetite for the things of God and things which take place in the Kingdom of God can be awakened. This is why we take individuals from one level of God to the next level of God's glory. This will cause them to experience new dimensions in God.

With children, you may take them on sight-seeing tours to the airport to see an airplane take off. Let them envision themselves going places, other than the park across the street. Sometimes our vision needs to be expanded. We think too small. This is one of the reasons we do not see great things take place in our lives.

We must dare to believe. I heard a prophetic word several years ago saying, "The move of the Spirit will be among the young, not the old because the old will keep on in the same path, but the generation I am raising up will build in a way that never has been seen, nor will ever be seen again."

Noah built for a day that he had never seen and a day that would not be seen again. Most of us are stuck on the "Give me that old time religion" song, so we are not able to build for days we haven't seen. We don't like to walk in the unfamiliar.

God likes to take a blind man and lead him in a place he has never known. The worst thing you can do to a blind man is to bring him into his living room, that he was once familiar with, after you have totally rearranged the furniture. You will cause the senses that he has developed to move around in that environment to become unreliable. God likes to put a blind man (we walk by faith, not by sight) in a situation where he cannot rely on himself, but on God and Him alone.

Jesus encouraged Peter to walk in the unfamiliar. Peter had never walked on water. Most of us criticize Peter, focusing on the fact that Peter sunk. Yet we need to preach about the eleven who stayed in the boat. When was the last time you walked on water? Peter was a voice used at Pentecost, because God saw that he dared to step out into the unfamiliar.

The purpose of renewing our minds is so we can

prove that which is the good, acceptable, and perfect will of God. You may be thinking, "How do I find God's will for my life?" The answer is by finding His Word. His Word is His will. His will is His Word. We are never told to find God's will, but to *prove* His will. We are too busy searching for the will of God, instead of proving the will of God.

Many people are praying for more power. Not one of us needs more power, because God has already given us the Holy Ghost. We need to utilize the power He has already given us. He has given us His Name. He has given us His Word. God has placed us in this world to change the complexion of it from doom and gloom to light and glory!

"Arise, shine; for thy light is come, and the glory of the Lord is risen upon thee"

(Isaiah 60:1).

God comes into our world precisely when there is confusion, chaos, and darkness. He begins to change us by the light of His Word, just as He gave the commandment at creation, *"Let there be light."*

Chapter 2
Your Mind: The Avenue Of Transformation

It is in the mind that transformation is needed to cause us to take on the image of Christ. Yet, the mind is also Satan's greatest battleground for keeping us from becoming like Christ.

> "...If any man be in Christ, he is a new creature: old things are passed away; behold, all things are become new"

(II Corinthians 5:17).

Yet, if our physical features were distorted before coming to Christ, they will be distorted after coming to Christ. If our feet were big before Christ, they will be big after coming to Christ. The only thing that changes when we are born-again is our spirit man. Our spirit man becomes alive unto God.

Battles are won or lost in the arena of the mind. For this reason, there must be a deprogramming of the mind before there can be a reprogramming of the life.

Weak men will produce weak families and if that is not corrected, weak families will begin to produce a weak church. In looking at this scenario, we also see that the cycle will continue and a weak church will produce weak nations.

While we were in the process of purchasing our church building, the Lord said unto me, "Begin to deal with the men of the house, and you will be able to purchase the land." I met regularly with the men, teaching them how to take their rightful place in the home, and how to be set free from fear and bondage. We were able to purchase the building.

The mind is the avenue of transformation. Romans 12:1-2, reinforces this fact.

The J. B. Phillips translation reads:

"With eyes wide open to the mercies of God, I beg you, brothers, as an act of intelligent worship, to give Him your bodies, as a living sacrifice, consecrated to him and acceptable by him."

Don't let the world around you squeeze you into its mold, but let God redesign you so that your whole attitude of mind is changed. Thus, you will prove, in practice, that the will of God is good, acceptable to Him, and perfect.

If you are not transformed in your mind, it is not God's

18

fault, it is not your neighbor's fault, nor is it your pastor's fault. It is solely your fault, because you have not purposed to renew your mind with God's Word.

The renewal (or transformation) of the mind takes place by meditating upon the Word of God.

We see this clearly in Joshua 1:8, *"This book of the law shall not depart out of thy mouth, but thou shalt meditate therein day and night, that thou mayest observe to do according to all that is written therein: for then thou shalt make thy way prosperous, and then thou shalt have good success."*

We are to meditate upon the Word of God day and night. When we meditate upon something, we chew on it like a cow chews his cud. A cow has four stomachs. Cows and sheep both chew cud. They store their food in the first compartment of their stomachs. Later, they regurgitate it, and then chew some more, breaking it down smaller before they swallow it again. Later, they regurgitate that same cud, continuing to chew it into even more digestible pieces.

Revelation (digesting) of the Word takes place in this same way. God gives us a Scripture, and we meditate upon it.

For example, Psalms 23:1 says, *"The Lord is my shepherd; I shall not want."*

We might focus (chew) on the fact that He is Jehovah Jireh, the Lord who provides. He is our shepherd. Then we swallow that and regurgitate it up again. We think (chew) on Him being our Shepherd. We look at the One

19

who leads us in the way of green pastures.

We meditate on the fact that He is the One who leads and guides us into all truth. We look at the Great Shepherd, wo loves us with an everlasting love. We look at Jesus, the One who leads us by the way of the still waters.

As we meditate upon this verse and digest it, suddenly the Word comes up, *"The Lord is my Shepherd. I shall not want."* The Holy Spirit may have us focus on, "I shall not want." When we learn who we are connected with, in contact with, and in relationship with, we will know that all of our needs are met, according to His riches in glory. We will know He is our Shepherd. We will say, "I have no want for anything. It has already been promised to me, because all the promises of God are yea and Amen."

When we meditate upon the Word of God, He will give us a revelation.

John received a revelation, and he said, *"...Behold the Lamb of God, which taketh away the sin of the world!"* (John 1:29).

This is an example of meditation. We keep muttering the Word over to ourselves. When we meditate upon the Word during the day, that will be the end of our nightmares, because that which we meditate upon in the day is the thing we will dream about at night.

Joshua said, *"...that thou mayest observe to do according to all that is written therein..."*

20

It is one thing to be a hearer of the Word. It is another thing to be a doer of it. For example, it is not enough just to hear the Word on giving. Giving is a way of life. You are to become a doer of the Word in this area.

If you want to reap everyday, you must learn how to give everyday. You cannot receive daily, unless you give daily.

When we counsel people who are having problems in their finances, the first thing we do is ask for a record of their giving. We have found that if they stopped giving in January, February, and March, and they started tithing again in April, May, June, and July, then suddenly in August, they start having a rough time financially. They say, "I don't understand. I have been giving." We explain to them that we noticed, according to our records, that during this period you were not giving. You are looking for a harvest to come, and you didn't plant anything during that time.

Joshua continues, "...for then thou shalt make thy way prosperous, and then thou shalt have good success." You are the one who makes your way prosperous.

Most of us want to shift the responsibility to someone else. "I can't help it. I was born this way. I couldn't do anything about it. I come from four generations of people who received government assistance, so it's just in my destiny to receive." You don't have to accept these lies!

Poverty is a state of mind. It is not determined by how much money we have. If we think poor, we will live poor. People with a poverty mentality are usually very negative in their approach towards life. If you are on welfare, God's principles, if obeyed, can cause you to get off of it. Welfare is not God's will. God wants you to say fare well to welfare!

Many of us have experienced an occasional lack of cash flow, but we know it is temporary. You can give a poor man a million dollars, and he will still be impoverished, because of his thinking. His mind has not been transformed.

There must be a deprogramming of the poverty mentality. God wants to deprogram us. He wants to change the way we think. He wants to get us out of the place where we no longer give as paupers, but where we give as kings.

It is God's will for us to live in abundance. That's part of the covenant. God wants His people to look prosperous. God wants us to have the best.

The sinner is in the earth for one of two reasons: either to get saved and come into the Kingdom, or for us to receive wealth of him, *"...and the wealth of the wicked is laid up for the righteous"* (Proverbs 13:22).

Fashioned After God's Kingdom

Now I would ask you, "What does it mean to be conformed to this world?" God's Word warns us not to be fashioned after or fall into the external and fleeting fashions of this age. Paul is saying, "I want you to go through a deep inner change." We need to be changed on the inside.

A child learns in one of three methods:

1) By observation: watching and mimicking the parent.

2) By explanation: You clarifying things for him.

3) By participation: Actually involving him in a process.

The Church needs to teach people by observation. We are to exhibit something to the world and to believers in Christ that they can mimic in their own lives. I don't believe that the people of the world are the ones to be looked upon as models. The example for mimicking needs to come from the Kingdom of God. The people of the Church have erroneously been told that the poorer we are, the holier we are.

Many of us have been told that in order to be sanctified or maintain a valid experience with Jesus, we need to maintain an austere, mediocre existence upon this earth. This is not Biblical truth. If Jesus walked the earth today in person, some people would have problems with Him. Did you know Jesus wore the best garments of His day? The Bible says He wore fine linen, and that the soldiers who crucified Him cast lots for His garments. Jesus wasn't poor, He was wealthy. Jesus called 12 men off of their jobs, provided for their daily needs, took care of their families, ministered to the poor and placed a thief, Judas, over the treasury! Some men can hardly call their wives off the job.

Jesus said that the man who does not take care of his home is worse than an infidel (I Timothy 5:8). We must fashion ourselves according to the Word, but first we must have our minds renewed.

Patriarchal Rule: God's Order

Our minds need to be renewed even as far as God's order concerning a man's role and impact upon our social structure. Many men have totally neglected and abdicated their ordained sphere of authority as patriarchal fathers. It is a curse upon our people to be under matriarchal rule. Exodus 6:3, does not say that God is the God of Sarah, Rebekah, and Rachel. In this Scripture, God is referred to as "a God of magistrates." Magistrates, according to Webster's dictionary, refers to "a civil officer empowered to administer the law."

The call of authority and rule is upon the patriarch to administer the law unto his family. God is the God of Abraham, Isaac, and Jacob!

Matriarchal rule always arises whenever a patriarch abdicates his throne, ceases to fulfill his role and responsibility, and forces a woman to function in realms of responsibility and authority for which she was never created.

Many of today's married women have had to become the primary providers for their homes to prevent total destruction of the family unit. Now, I am not addressing the woman who is working by choice or the single woman. I am specifically referring to the woman who finds herself assuming the headship of the family unit due to the willful neglect, irresponsibility, laziness, or ineptitude of her husband.

Any man who shuns his responsibility as caretaker of his family and puts that burden upon his wife has embraced castration as a way of life. As men, all we need to do to avoid this type of situation is to enter into covenant with God and be like Abraham, who placed his confidence and trust in God to prosper him and had the testimony, *"No man has made me rich but Almighty God"* (Genesis 14:23).

God will make you a prophetic father. He will make you a patriarch where the Word of the Lord will come in your mouth and you will bring the household into direction and order, because direction is to come down from the head. It is not a superior or inferior type of thing. It is just the order and the structure that God has separated and sanctified.

I was talking to a lawyer recently and he said, "Most men do not become real men until about the age of 35. They begin to wake up and say, 'You know, I should buy a house instead of getting another car.'

In Jewish culture, at the age of 13, the young boys go through a ceremony that says, "You are no longer a boy. You are now a man."

In European culture, many young men are not on the basketball court during the summer. Instead, they are in the workforce learning responsibility and making the transition from boyhood to manhood.

In African culture, when young men are 12 or 13, they go through the right of passage. They go with the older men, who take them from boyhood to manhood, teaching them that they are coming to an age of responsibility.

It is imperative that the Church begins to set a godly example of patriarchal fathers to stimulate the development of our next generation of young men.

From Glory to Glory

God's plan is to take us from glory to glory, and this can happen only when our minds are renewed by meditating in the Word of God. Only then will we think and act like Jesus.

In the Old Testament, there was a glory on the law, but because of the glory that excelleth, it seemed as though there was no glory on it. There is a glory on all the past moves of God, but now there is a glory that excelleth. That is why God takes us from glory to glory.

> *"For even that which was made glorious had no glory in this respect, by reason of the glory that excelleth.*
>
> *For if that which is done away was glorious, much more that which remaineth is glorious.*
>
> *Seeing then that we have such hope, we use great plainness of speech:*
>
> *And not as Moses, which put a veil over his face, that the children of Israel could not steadfastly look to the end of that which is abolished".*

(II Corinthians 3:10-13).

We can see that Moses put a veil on his face because the Israelites could not look upon the glory that rested on him after he had been with God.

There are godly leaders today who are veiled, because the people are not willing to look upon them and see God's glory.

II Corinthians 3:14 says, *"But their minds were blinded: for until this day remaineth the same veil untaken away in the reading of the old testament; which veil is done away in Christ."*

I believe the very thing that was on Moses' face was Christ. Christ simply means "the anointed One." The Israelites would not enter into the Presence of the anointed One. They would not partake of Him, and because of that, Moses had to wear a veil and deal with the people from a distance. Today, there are so many that be in the Body of Christ who want a relationship with the Lord, but they want it from a distance.

Some people say, "Lord, save me through and through, but don't tell me what to do with my money." Jesus is either Lord of all, or He is not Lord at all! On one occasion, Jesus told the rich young ruler, "Sell all you have and give it to the poor so you can enter into My Kingdom," but the rich young ruler couldn't part with his possessions to obtain the wealth of salvation.

There is a difference in knowing Jesus as Savior and knowing Him as Lord. You can know Him as Savior saying, "Lord Jesus, come into my life. I receive You." It's another thing to know Him as Lord, because when you know Him as Lord, He is Lord of *all*.

Herod and Pilate had no problem with Jesus' priestly ministry, and Satan doesn't have a problem with you entering into the priestly ministry of Jesus. He says, "Yes, just love Jesus. Worship Him. Just love the Lord, but stay within your four walls, stay inside of the church, go ahead and sing. There's nothing wrong with that. I have no objection to the priestly ministry of Jesus."

Matthew 2:2 says, "...*Where is he that is born King of the Jews?....*"

Notice, they did not say, "Where is He that is priest of the Jews"? They didn't make a mockery of His priestly ministry, but they mocked His kingly ministry. The devil doesn't care how much you become a worshipper of God, how much you enter into the holy priesthood, but he doesn't want you to enter into the royal priesthood. He doesn't want you to move into that kingly anointing, because that means you will take ground he thinks is his. You will decree things and they will be so.

II Corinthians 3:15-18

"But even unto this day, when Moses is read, the veil is upon their heart.

Nevertheless, when it shall turn to the Lord, the veil shall be taken away.

Now the Lord is that Spirit: and where the Spirit of the Lord is, there is liberty.

But we all, with open face beholding as in a glass the glory of the Lord, are changed into the same image from glory to glory, even as by the Spirit of the Lord."

What image are we beholding? As we behold the Lord, we are changed into the same image of the glory of the Lord. This means, if we stare at pornographic magazines and saturate ourselves with soap operas, the very thing we behold will become a part of us.

Television promotes the "world's" image of women. It shows the woman in the executive office, wearing a mink coat being escorted in a limousine. She flashes an American Express card and sits down to dinner with a glass of wine. Then, in contrast, they show the housewife with a mop! The god of this age makes a mockery of women who stay home to care for their children.

The whole aspect of two incomes is really a myth, because when you have a double income, you usually have the additional expense of babysitting fees, transportation, clothes, hair styling, dry cleaning expense, and lunch money.

Now, don't quote me as being against women working, but I believe God wants every man to reach up and get a vision for his family. I believe it is in the mind of God for every man to have his own enterprise so that his family can work in it. So many of the things we do are contrary to God's plan.

Every major war that has ever taken place has been over real estate. That is why we find that wealth is connected to real estate. The only thing that is real is the earth, and it is the Lord's (Psalm 24:1). The devil doesn't want you to occupy the land.

We worked diligently to burn the mortgage on our

church building. I have found that if people can't see God provide for His own house (the Church facilities), they will never be able to see Him provide for their own houses.

When Noah got ready to build an ark, God did not say, "Go float a loan."

Your mind is being renewed right now, if you will listen to what God is speaking. He wants us debt free.

The very thing that we imagine or meditate upon is the thing that is grafted into our souls. It becomes a part of our lives. That's why we must understand that everything we hear is either making a deposit or a withdrawal from our lives.

When you go to the bank, you either make a deposit or a withdrawal. Whatever you look at is either making a deposit into your life or a withdrawal from it.

If you are having a problem in a certain area of your mind or in an area of your flesh, then you know there are certain movies you have no business watching. You need to discern what you watch on TV.

The Imagination and Transformation

It has been said that the imagination is the mirror of the soul. It is the place where you take old thoughts and new thoughts and merge them together to form new ideas. The imagination or imagery is the picture power of the mind. We can see mental images and pictures.

Your purpose is found in the imagination, because the Holy Spirit places a thought and causes it to incubate in the mind. You will never have leadership, initiative, self-confidence, or purpose until it is first created in your imagination. You must see yourself possessing these things before they become a reality.

The mind has two roles: It has the ability to play back. This means that the mind has the ability to form mental pictures of events or happenings of the past that have been stored in the subconscious. It also has the ability to play forward. The imagination allows the mind to forecast and deal with future problems, as well as create something never before seen, such as an invention or an event.

The imagination is the workshop of the mind. It is a place of creativity, a place of calculation, a place of reckoning, a place of consideration, and a place of reflection.

Some imaginations are wasted, because we don't meditate on the right things. First, meditate on the Word of God. God's Word must be preeminent in our minds. We need to sleep, and eat the Word daily.

I never allow my mind to sit on "idle." My mind is constantly working on something. The Holy Spirit is continually creating in my mind. The Holy Spirit wants to work in your mind.

Scripture says darkness was upon the face of the deep, and the Spirit of God moved upon the face of the water (Genesis 1:2). God wants to move upon the face of the deep of your mind, which is full of darkness and chaos, and cause light to come in and bring

31

understanding, comprehension, and creative ideas that have never existed.

I believe God wants to change our heaven and earth by first beginning a work in us. *Father, let Thy will be done in earth (in me) as it is in heaven.*

Is there any sickness in heaven? Of course not! Then sickness has no place in us. Is there any poverty in heaven? No! So poverty has no place in us. Let Thy will be done in the earth, O Lord, as it is in heaven! Therefore, whatever is going on in heaven, or whatever heaven represents, that is what we are to represent in our earthen vessels.

Many defeats and failures are due to mental blindness and moral deviations. If you live only by physical sight, your world will be very small. Our world extends only as far as we can see. When God spoke to Abraham about multiplying his seed, He told Him to look at the stars and at the sand. He began to redirect his focus. We need to take our children outside of our neighborhoods and give them an opportunity to see other things. Make that investment in their lives. Teach them to read about other things.

We see with our mind, as well as with our eyes. Our eyes are only a pair of windows that we use to perceive our surroundings. Our minds assimilate the sum of our perceptions and categorizes the information to enhance our comprehension.

Moses sent out 12 spies to peruse the Promised Land. All 12 saw the same thing, but they came back with two different reports. They all looked out of the same pair of windows, but ten saw themselves as grasshoppers and the opposition as giants. The other two said, "Man, they are bread enough for us to eat."

Two came back with a good report, while ten came back with an evil report. Why? They saw out of the same pair of windows, but they all saw something different in their minds. We see with our minds, not with our eyes. That's why the key is in the renewing of the mind. Our sight begins to change, and it changes the focal point of what we look at.

Some of us are looking at the numbers in our bank book. I've heard many people caution us to keep a balanced attitude towards prosperity. The only balance I know is when I have a deficit in my checking account, I need some prosperity to bring up the balance! *Quick!* I talk a lot about whatever the Bible talks about, and it talks money from Genesis to Revelation. Money is a neutral force, and we are the ones who determine whether it is righteous or wicked.

The Scripture tells in Ecclesiastes 10:19, that money has a language of its own. That means it has the ability to talk. If you don't respect money, it will not respect you. A close friend of mine said, "I will not talk money among you until you all learn how to respect money. Money is something you must learn to respect, but not love it where it exceeds your love for God."

Money is not the root of all evil, but the "love of it" is what gets us in trouble. A lot of poor people who don't

have money have a love of money. They will do anything to get it. When we understand that money is actually a spiritual force, it will gravitate toward us.

The Bible says that wisdom is your sister. It says wisdom cries out in the streets. We are to embrace wisdom.
Wisdom finds knowledge of witty inventions. A short-
age of money usually isn't a money problem. It is an
idea problem. All we need to do is learn how to tap into
the Holy Ghost. He will give us good ideas, and money
chases good ideas, which are a God-given wisdom.

MEDITATION-The Key To Unlock New Horizons In God

Your Mind: The Avenue Of Transformation

Chapter 3
Beholding the Grapes

Pray aloud with me now: FATHER, I THANK YOU FOR GIVING ME A SEEING EYE AND A HEARING EAR, FOR TOUCHING MY MIND AND CAUSING IT TO BE RENEWED BY THE WORD OF THE LORD.

I THANK YOU, FATHER, THAT NO LONGER WILL I SEE GIANTS. NO LONGER WILL I HAVE A GRASSHOPPER COMPLEX, BUT I AM GOING TO SEE THE GRAPES. I AM GOING TO SEE THE VICTORY. ALL MY NEEDS ARE MET ACCORDING TO YOUR RICHES IN GLORY.

I THANK YOU, LORD, THAT RIGHT NOW YOU ARE TOUCHING MY MIND. YOU ARE CHANGING MY FOCUS, YOU ARE CAUSING ME TO SEE THE THINGS I AM TO SEE. I BLESS YOU FOR IT NOW IN JESUS' NAME. AMEN.

Begin to rejoice and thank the Lord for all the mighty things He is doing! Every time we hear a report, someone is either talking about giants or grapes. Joshua and Caleb focused on the cluster of grapes, while the ten that came back with the evil report focused on the giants.

Sometimes all we do is focus on the giants, and we have a poor self image. We have a defeatist or a poverty mentality. I refuse to accept poverty. Poverty not only has a certain look, but it has a certain smell.

When I enter a room, I can smell poverty. Stinginess sits on the borderline of poverty. Nothing goes out from the hand of the person who is impoverished, therefore, nothing can come in.

When you become a cheerful giver, you rejoice in God for your gift. You learn how to give freely, because you learn that God created you as a channel for giving.

When people come to Jesus, we teach them how to give. God so loved the world that He gave. He gave His only Son, but look how many sons He is reaping today!

We are dealing with renewal of the mind. Some people making $60,000 a year may have a poverty mentality. The only difference between them and someone on welfare is they are broke on a higher level.

If we need a million dollars to do the work of the Lord, we will not need to look outside of our perimeters. God will use what is in our presence to meet the need. Wherever God guides, He provides. He meets the need by what is in our midst.

Whatever God calls you to do, that which you need will gravitate toward you, enabling you to fulfill His plan.

When the woman was created, she was created equal to the man. They moved together as heirs. God created the family to be a community of authority.

After the fall of man, the role of the man and woman changed because of sin. The wife's desire is to be toward her husband. In the Hebrew, this means "she desires to rule over the man". I was amazed when I traced this! Every woman looks for a good man. I find that women challenge men to see how strong they are and if the man continues to give in to the wife, she understands that she doesn't have a man.

Not only does this affect your life, but it affects generations after you, because you reproduce the same spirit in your seed.

This is the manner in which the eagle operates. When the eagle begins to fly, she looks for a mate. Those of you who are looking for a mate, take a lesson from this illustration! She goes up in the clouds and if there is a male eagle that wants to mate with her, she takes a branch and drops it. If the male eagle grabs the branch, then they keep flying. She then gets a heavier branch and takes it to the sky. Again, she drops it to see if the male eagle can grab it and keep going. She will get a heavier branch the third time, and when she drops it, if he cannot catch it, she won't mate with him. It seems like the eagle has more insight than some Christians!

This is what God wants to instill into the people of God. Often, we find individuals who compromise and later become sorry. They bring forth a family, and instead of a family with a patriarchal rule, there is a strong matriarchal rule.

It is easy to discern a wife who has the spirit of a matriarch. If I am talking to a husband and wife and the wife always interrupts her husband, this demonstrates an attitude of disrespect toward her husband. When it is reproduced between two parents, the children will show that same disrespect, and it is perpetuated generation after generation. All of this is involved in the renewing of the mind. God wants us to understand these principles of the kingdom.

We become whatever we see, whatever we look at, and whatever our mind envisions. Whatever images come before us, those are the things we become.

Sometimes we look at the world of finance as an inconquerable giant. It seems as though the money needed is just too great. Fear causes us to focus on the giants, instead of seeing the grapes the Father sent us after. God wants us to move from the perspective of focusing on the giants to focusing on the grapes.

I learned some valuable principles from a book that talked about laying on of hands to invoke the Father's blessings.

The Orthodox Jewish tradition is that the senior patriarch lays his hands on the children to invoke God's blessings upon them. Thank God for praying mothers, but we need to receive and encourage praying fathers who are invoking the blessings of God upon their children.

As we come into a knowledge of truth, we clearly see that men must be raised up to do the work God has called them to do so that they will have a strong influence upon their seed. When you destroy the man, you destroy the seed. You destroy the race.

We need to take a fresh lesson from Proverbs 31 regarding the wife. Everything she undertook and accomplished revolved around her home.

There are principles in God's Kingdom concerning the home and the family. I believe the lethal judgment of AIDS has come upon the earth because the hearts of the fathers have not been turned toward their children. Since children have not found their father's love, they have looked for it in other relationships (ungodly relationships) which have resulted in homosexuality and promiscuity. It is sad that many children have been deprived of a father's love. Many sons have never experienced being embraced by their fathers.

The lack of emotional bonding between the father and son leaves an innate desire within the son for a father's love. When this desire is unfilled, a void is created in the son that yearns to be satisfied by the embrace of a man.

It has been scientifically proven that fathers who have shown great amounts of affection to their sons, have raised sons who are not distorted or twisted in relationships. Neither do they have a problem becoming trans-

41

parent in life. The reverse is true when the fathers did not show affection to their sons. These very issues are the root of whether people focus on the giants (challenges) of life or whether they are free to focus on the grapes (the harvest or the good report).

This is why I believe God is raising up Christians schools. Christians are the ones who are to be teaching sex education. Today, adolescents make fun of their peers who are still virgins. We see people giving up their virginity, giving up the very thing that God has given them. God sent them to earth as a sealed package and that seal is not to be broken until they meet their mates. Our young people need to be taught the sacredness of virginity, and the purpose for it.

Our young men need to be taught that their manhood is not determined by how many women submit to them. They need to be taught that the seed that God has given them is sacred and that their behavior today will affect future generations.

In praying and seeking for a mate, take note that if you find a man who disrespects his mother, you will have problems with him in marriage, because if he has no respect for his mother, he won't have any respect for you. Similarly, if you marry a young lady who disrespects her father and she has a problem with male authority, what makes you think she will love you so much that you will be able to change her?

We find that the degree of a person's submission will determine the degree of authority in his life. If you were a person who has never submitted to authority, you will never be appointed to stand in authority.

Generally, you have to be under authority before God will make you an individual of authority. God will purposely place you under tutors and governors until the time appointed of the Father.

Dethroning Wrong Thoughts

"Casting down imaginations, and every high thing that exalteth itself against the knowledge of God, and bringing into captivity every thought to the obedience of Christ."

(2 Corinthians 10:5).

The above Scripture tells us how to dethrone wrong thoughts that have nested in our minds.

Some of us have been so trained that when we shop for clothes, the first thing we look at is the price tag rather than at what we like. I don't think anyone gets better buys than I do. I always know what I want, and I know how to work through the channel to get what I want. I look for what I want, then I walk out with it.

I went into a store one day looking for several suits. The salesman quoted an astronomical price for the suits. I said to him, "That is not the price I have in mind." I told him I felt as though God said for me to spend a certain amount in this store today. He looked at me as if I were crazy, but the end of the story is that I purchased the suits for the amount I had in my mind.

The Holy Spirit will teach you how to shop. He will give you wisdom. He will teach you how to buy furniture, clothes, food, etc. He will show you how to get the best for less. We can only do that, however, if we are operating the principles of the Kingdom, such as paying our tithes and giving offerings.

Not too long ago, a brother approached me and said, "I have a Mercedes I am going to give to you. I asked, "Is it any good?" That was my natural mind talking! (Assuming something had to be wrong with it). He responded, "It's an excellent car."

God was speaking in a man's spirit telling him to sow a vehicle. Can you imagine that our God would do that? But I am always giving, and the Bible says, *"Give, and it shall be given unto you; good measure, pressed down, and shaken together, and running over..."* Who shall give to you? *Men* shall give unto your bosom (Luke 6:38).

II Corinthians 10:3-4 says:

"For though we walk in the flesh, we do not war after the flesh. (For the weapons of our warfare are not carnal, but mighty through God to the pulling down of strongholds)."

We do not fight the devil with natural weapons. To pull down strongholds, we have to use the weapons of the Lord.

We must learn to captivate all the thoughts in our minds. We must learn to bring every thought under the Lordship of Jesus Christ. God's provision comes as we obey His commands. Jesus spoke to the ten lepers, "Go show yourself to the priest." They were not healed until they went. In the natural mind, for a leper to show himself unto the priest was suicide, because an unclean leper would be stoned to death. But the Bible says they were healed as they went, as they took each step of faith, they believed the word of the Master, Jesus.

When the pastor asks one of his parishioners to do something, there should be no question about it. If you were in the military service and an officer said to you, "We want you to go over there," you wouldn't respond, "Oh, I have to check in my spirit. I don't feel led, officer." You wouldn't do that, so why do we do it in the Kingdom of God?

How do we take thoughts captive? By taking another thought that is much more powerful and putting that thought in its place.

If your mind is filled with lying, then you need to fill your mind with truth. That's why I don't understand why some preachers preach so hard against homosexuality, fornication and adultery, and their church is filled with it. The more they preach on it, the more these people are drawn to that church. Why? Because that is what is being magnified. They continually put before them fornication, homosexuality, and adultery. That is the image that is being placed in their minds instead of the image of Jesus Christ.

We think in pictures. That which we meditate upon becomes a part of us. Therefore, we must cast down, or bring every thought into captivity or into obedience to Christ.

II Corinthians 10:6 says,

"And having in a readiness to revenge all disobedience, when your obedience is fulfilled."

The only way you revenge disobedience is when you are obedient. The Church will be able to expand the Kingdom of God only when they, themselves, begin to be obedient to the King.

Submission to Authority

Webster's dictionary defines submission as "to yield oneself to the authority or will of another". Submitting to authority does not mean to be in bondage. Authority is specified jurisdiction delegated by God to function and bring order.

My head is on my body, and the purpose of the head is to bring coordination, direction, and instruction. My head doesn't look at my feet and say, "I am the head. You listen to me." The feet automatically know to listen to the head to stay in coordination.

Because we have not understood authority for the purpose of order and protection, we look at authority as, "They are just trying to control me." My hands do not say, "That head is always trying to control me. I am just going to break off from the body."

You can readily identify an individual who is not under authority. They are sad, and they are into everything. They make a mess of everything they get into, because they can't find their head. They are completely out of order.

When you look at the order of the Kingdom, it is first God, the family, the Church, and then the job.

When the head of the chicken is chopped off, the chicken still has a little bit of life in it and it begins to flip around. It goes around in circles, running around the yard headless, and unaware of its impending death. That's how we are when we are dislocated from the head, and Jesus Christ is the Head of the Church.

The anointing does not qualify authority. You can be anointed, but still be out from under authority. You have to stay in the local assembly that God has set you in until you understand how the vision He has given you fits into the corporate vision of the Body. Any time your part becomes more important than the whole, you will miss the entire purpose of God.

Anointing does not qualify ministry. David was anointed as a shepherd boy, then he was anointed as king, but that did not qualify him to function as a king at that moment. There's a difference between the call and the separation. Everyone who is called to do something is not immediately separated unto it.

I was called as a prophet from my mother's womb, but that didn't mean they were to take me, sit me up there, and put a collar around my neck at two years old and say, "He is a prophet." I wasn't separated to function as one yet, though I was called from the womb.

Many people have been called, but God hasn't put His stamp of approval for separation on them yet. What you do between the call and the separation will determine whether or not you will ever be separated.

A couple of years ago, we heard the Spirit of God say, "The days of wandering minstrels are over." We call them "tumbleweed".

The Bible says we are "...*tossed to and fro and carried about with every wind of doctrine...*" (Ephesians 4:14).

Tumbleweed dwells in the desert, and it is tossed to and fro and is moved by every wind. If they hear "prosperity", they run in that direction, and is they hear"prophetic", off they go again in a vain pursuit for fulfillment. They blow with every wind of doctrine. Instead of signs following them, they follow signs. The Bible says, "These signs shall follow them that believe." The reason signs don't follow some people is because they are not going anywhere. You must be going somewhere in order for something to follow you.

Tumbleweed is not planted, and it bears no fruit. There isn't any life in it. Tumbleweed lacks covering and is aimlessly blown about, subject to the intense extremes of the elements. A person who is "blown about" will lack the spiritual covering necessary to protect them from the heated onslaughts of the enemy. Some people in the Church are like tumbleweed. They are not planted, and they are not bearing fruit. The Bible says we are to be as

48

trees planted by the Lord. More people leave churches for the wrong reason. Have you noticed that trees do not plan themselves? We need to teach, "Plant not thyself."

Many people who leave churches are running from the dealings of God. Yet, they can't avoid Him, for His dealings will be waiting for them when they get to the next church! Have you noticed that the trees do not get up and move when the neighborhood goes down? "Well, you know, they are not showing enough love to me on this block, so I am going to get up and move...they don't appreciate my ministry. They don't even thank me for giving them shade, so I think I am going to get up and move to the next block where they will appreciate me a little more."

We are supposed to be trees of righteousness, but many of us get up and leave when things are not going well. The planting of the Lord is able to withstand the pressures of growth without becoming uprooted.

Hebrews 12:1-2 says:

"Wherefore, seeing we also are compassed about with so great a cloud of witnesses, let us lay aside every weight, and the sin which doth so easily beset us, and let us run with patience the race that is set before us.

Looking unto Jesus, the author and finisher of our faith, who for the joy that was set before him endured the cross, despising the shame, and is set down at the right hand of the throne of God."

Jesus did not focus on the cross, He focused on the joy. If you can focus in the joy of that which God is bringing you into, you will be able to endure the cross. The reason many people are not able to endure is because they focus on their problems and circumstances rather than on the joy that is set before them.

They focus on the giants instead of the grapes. If they would focus on the grapes, they would be able to endure and conquer the giants.

Jesus is the leader, and He never focused on the cross. In the Garden of Gethsemane He said, *"Not My will, but Thine be done."* He looked beyond the suffering to the will of the Father.

Sometimes God asks us to do something. I was in a meeting and God told me to write a check for $1,000. I said, "Lord, You know I've got this and that to do." God knew what I had to do before He told me to write the check!

What happens is we don't focus on the joy of that which God is about to bring forth, and we are not able to endure the cross. God wants us to get the image of the joy that is set before us. Instead of focusing on the giants, we need to focus on the grapes.

Then, too, we need to have a destination. When we go to the airport, the first thing they ask is, "Where would like to go?" We must have a destination. If we say, "I just want to fly in a plane," they will not give us a ticket to an unspecified destination. We must have a destination in life.

Maybe you have been singing:

"One day at a time, sweet Jesus

That's all I'm asking from you.

So just give me the strength,

All I want is just one day at a time."

We need more than one day at a time! When Jesus came to earth, He came with a mission. He knew exactly what He was to do.

In Luke 2, Jesus went to Jerusalem with His parents for the feast of the passover. Jesus was 12 at the time, and when His parents left Jerusalem, they did not know that Jesus tarried behind. When they discovered that Jesus was not with them, they returned to Jerusalem in search of Him. After three days, they found Him.

> *"And when they saw him, they were amazed: and his mother said unto him, Son, why hast thou thus dealt with us? behold, thy father and I have sought thee sorrowing.*
>
> *And he said unto them, How is it that ye sought me wist ye not that I must be about my Father's business? And they understood not the saying which he spake unto them.*
>
> *And he went down with them, and came to Nazareth, and was subject unto them: but his mother kept all these sayings in her heart.*
>
> *And Jesus increased in wisdom and stature, and in favour with God and man".*

(Luke 2:48-52).

Notice, Verse 51 says that Jesus was subject to His parents. That means He submitted to their authority. We must learn how to become subject, because when the time of release comes, God knows how to get in touch with those who are in authority over us to say, "Release them. They are Mine."

I believe it was because of Jesus' subjection to authority that He "increased in wisdom and stature, and in favour with God and man." Likewise, if we want to grow in wisdom and stature and in favor with God and man, we must be subject to authority. That is a vital characteristic of one who goes for the grapes - God's highest - and wins!

MEDITATION-The Key To Unlock New Horizons In God

Beholding The Grapes

Chapter 4
Taking Thoughts Captive

"For though we walk (live) in the flesh, we are not carrying on our warfare according to the flesh and using mere human weapons.

For the weapons of our warfare are not physical [weapons of flesh and blood], but they are mighty before God for the overthrow and destruction of strongholds.

[Inasmuch as we] refute arguments and theories and reasonings and every proud and lofty thing that sets itself up against the [true] knowledge of God: and we lead every thought and purpose away captive into the obedience of Christ (the Messiah, the Anointed One).

Being in readiness to punish every [insubordi-

nate for his] disobedience, when your own submission and obedience [as a church] are fully secured and complete.

(I Corinthians 10:3-6, AMP).

Let's look at some thoughts that are contrary to the nature and plan of God. Within our minds are particular grooves, and our minds often move in one groove. I believe the renewing of the mind comes when we cross the grooves. This is where the trouble begins. "I have always said it this way. This is the way my mother did it. This is the only way I know to do it." When we begin to cast these thoughts down and experience that which is unfamiliar, we begin to cross the grooves in our minds!

What the Father wants us to understand is that the renewal of the mind takes place when we are able to reroute our thinking processes and line them up with the direction of the Lord.

The first thing we must realize is that our minds are the battleground between truth and fallacy.

Most of the problems we will ever experience will be in the area of the unrenewed mind. God does not have a problem, because He never changes. He is always the same. Our problem is not with God, it is with ourselves. Often, we are so busy trying to fight the enemy on the outside, when our biggest enemy is within the arena of the mind.

A particular man of God began to tell people, "I know who the Antichrist is." They asked, "Who is the Antichrist?" He told them, "It's simple. It's that thing that sits between your two ears." We look for the Antichrist as being a man, but the Antichrist is anyone or anything that is ANTI-Christ. If your next door neighbor doesn't know Jesus, he is anti-Christ.

"And every spirit that confesseth not that Jesus Christ is come in the flesh is not of God: and this is that spirit of Antichrist, whereof ye have heard it should come; and even now is it in the world "

(I John 4:3)

Antichrist is not a 20th or 21st century theology. The spirit of Antichrist has been present since John's day. This is why we are working on getting our minds renewed, because an unrenewed mind is Anti-Christ.

Once people are born-again, they still do wrong or anti-Christ types of things. For instance, many people today are led by the Holy Spirit, yet they are not under authority.

Though Saul came against David, David still would not touch Saul. David knew God's guideline, *"...Touch not mine anointed, and do my prophets no harm"* (Psalm 105:15).

We need to realize that God wants us to understand, with clarity, that delegated authority and God are inseparable. When you touch delegated authority, you touch God. The thing that God looks at, even if the authority is in error, is the way we respond to authority.

Even when Daniel was placed in the den of lions, the next morning when they opened the den, he looked up and said, *"...O king, live for ever"* (Daniel 6:21). Daniel was a man who was under authority.

The three Hebrew boys didn't become bitter with the king either, but they submitted to authority. You see, there is a difference between submission and obedience. Obedience is an outward action, while submission is an attitude of the heart.

Because the three Hebrew boys [Shadrach, Meshach, and Abednego] were under authority, God gave them authority over the fire. The measure of your submission will determine the degree of your authority.

We need to understand spiritual protocol. It should not shock you to know that God has an order of authority and submission in the Spirit. There is an order for prophecy to come forth. Sometimes people give the right word, but they give it at the wrong time. Sometimes a musician plays a right note, but it is played at the wrong time, causing him to be out of tune. Many individuals are spiritually out of tune. They have the right word, but they bring it at the wrong time.

Our Father is going to teach us, in the renewing of the mind, the difference between time and the fullness of time.

You can be three months pregnant and deliver, but there is no way that baby can live. A lot of words

58

are delivered that are not living, because they are not birthed in the fullness of time. As a result, they don't make the impact that is needed.

Some of us don't want to go the full nine months. When my wife was about seven or eight months pregnant, she said, "I wish this child would come now," because of discomfort in the natural. But, you must wait for the fullness of time for the baby to be healthy.

There are individuals, as well as ministers who think they cannot wait until the fullness of time. They say, "We want it birthed now."

I am pregnant with revelation, but some revelation cannot come forth until the fullness of time. If it comes forth prematurely, it will be aborted.

"Casting down imaginations, and every high thing that exalteth itself against the knowledge of God, and bringing into captivity every thought to the obedience of Christ".

(I Corinthians 10:5)

The Greek word for thought is NOEMA. Your thoughts are an area of the mind that must be brought into captivity. They must be brought under the Lordship of Jesus Christ.

We are to cast down imaginations. Imaginations are the mirror of the soul.

In III John 2, we see that the prosperity of our outer man depends on the prosperity of our inner man (the soul). If our souls are not prospering, then we will not prosper in the external realm.

For years, I never understood how an individual could be a believer in the Lord Jesus Christ and not walk in prosperity. Then I realized that people came to a saving knowledge of Jesus Christ, but they never walked in the fullness of truth concerning developing the prosperity of their souls.

Often people say, "I've got Jesus and that's enough." Let me tell you, that's not enough. We need His Word.

James tells us to receive the engrafted Word, which is able to "save your soul." James was talking to believers. Why would he tell believers to receive the engrafted Word, which is able to save their souls? Our spirit is born-again when we are saved, but our souls are still unsaved. Our spirit man comes alive unto God when we are born-again, but our souls (mind) are not automatically saved. The mind is saved as it is fed by the Word of God.

That's why the Word says, "...and I pray God your whole spirit and soul and body be preserved blameless unto the coming of our Lord Jesus Christ" (I Thessalonians 5:23).

My mother used to make preserves. She put some pears in a jar, put a seal on them, and they would keep for years without spoiling.

I want to teach you how to preserve your soul. You can come into a particular doctrine in Christ. It might be a doctrine concerning healing, prosperity, or the family. You can receive the engrafted Word to such a degree until you set a seal on it and nothing will be able to spoil you in that area of your life.

That's why I tell people they can sit under the teaching of the Word in our church for six months, and we can get them off of welfare. We can teach them the Word of God concerning prosperity until it is so engrafted into their souls, then we can set the seal on it. Never again will they be spoiled in that area. No more poverty! You might have a cash flow problem now and then, but you will never know poverty again once your soul has been saved in that area.

We are going to touch another sacred cow.

In Proverbs 11:30, the Scripture says, *"he that winneth souls is wise."*

We thought that meant getting someone born-again. Just because a woman gives birth to a baby does not make her a mother, and just because a male plants a seed does not make him a father.

Many people are leading people into the salvation experience, but they are not getting their souls saved. A soul is saved when it receives the engrafted Word with meekness and comes into the fullness of the stature of Christ.

In other words, the bottom line is, "How many individuals have you discipled? How many have you brought into the fullness of the stature of Christ?" We probably should ask, "How many of you have sat under anyone long enough to come into the fullness of the stature of anything?

We also need to understand that the demon that operates in the Church called "my ministry" must bow to the Joseph principle: Our dream must die and we must work on the dreams of others that ours may live. If you don't work on the vision of another person, your vision will never come forth.

Before Jesus' disciples became apostles, they didn't say, "Listen, Jesus, I've been with You for a year, and You haven't really released me into the ministry. I am still picking up the fragments from the 5,000."

When Jesus numbered the strength of a church, He did it not by the degree of people who were there, but by the degree of men who were there. In Scripture, the multitude were 5,000 men, 7,000 men, 4,000 men, besides women and children, because the strength of a church is determined by the strength of men who are there. I believe there are a lot of men who have not yet reached up to receive the office of manhood.

The qualification of ministry is not established by anointing, but it is established by character. The Bible doesn't say, "By their gifts you shall know them." It says, "By their fruit you shall know them."

I can lay hands on you and impart gifts, but it takes time to grow fruit. The basis for ministry comes back to the family. If a man desires to be a bishop, an elder, or a leader in the Church, the Word says he is to be the husband of one wife and his wife and children are to be under subjection. His home is to be in order.

I have seen too many ministries where the man goes out in ministry and the wife goes to work to financially support it. That's not a principle of God's Kingdom. We are seeing too much of this in our culture. We must set a standard - God's standard.

We started a church with about five members, and we had a hotel bill to pay of about $800 a month for our meeting room. Don't ask me how God met it! I looked at our books sometime ago, and it amazed me! I don't know how the money came in! All I know is that it came in and we did not starve, because we had a covenant with God.

The thought never entered my mind, "Honey, you go out and work for the next couple of years until we are able to tide things over." No!! We had a covenant with God. She took care of our children, because the Bible says, "Every wise woman builds her house... (Proverbs 14:1)." Many people have houses, but they don't have a home. There is a difference.

I opened a business. I didn't have to get a loan. I did get a mortgage when we purchased our house, but I don't believe in getting loans for business. Too many people have gone bankrupt with business loans, especially if they were experimenting. Nevertheless, we started a business, and God continued to bless.

Then the Father began to speak to me about buying a building. The Holy Spirit said, "Buy that building." Now, this was the same Voice who told me what to give. The particular building was a shell. I went down to the city auction and bought the building. The price kept going up, but the Holy Ghost told me to buy it. He told me to buy a building I had never been in, which is not good business sense.

Within two weeks, the Holy Spirit again spoke to me and said, "Sell it." He told me a specific price to sell for, but we sold it far above the price and made over 100 percent profit. That is the power of the Holy Ghost!

Now, when I tell my wife, "Honey, we are going to do this or that," she says, "I know you hear from God." If she is not sure she says, "Honey, I don't know about that. I'll check it in my spirit again, but if that is what you feel to do, go right ahead with it." I have her confidence, because she has seen my track record with the Lord.

When I talk about patriarchal and matriarchal homes, you need to realize that I came out of a situation where my mother was the pillar of the home. If it wasn't for her, there wouldn't have been a home.

Even when things were difficult, I kept a smile on my face, and said, "Everything is fine. God is blessing." Why? Because of the covenant we had with God.

If I had never been tested by my previous struggles, I wouldn't be experiencing my present achievements. Your present day struggles are preparing you to handle tomorrow's achievements.

What does this have to do with renewing your mind and taking thoughts captive to the obedience of Christ? Everything!

The Word of God was our key to survival as we began to press into our covenant rights with God, and wherever you are today in your walk with the Lord, the Word is still your key.

Taking Thoughts Captive

Chapter 5
Prophetic Prescriptions for Effective Mind Renewal

If our minds are renewed through the Word of God, we will no longer get into some of the predicaments most of us have been in.

I have had people say to me, "Pastor, we need money to pay our rent." I do not give people money to pay their rent. If their rent is overdue, it is an indication that they are under judgment, not that they are in sin, but they are under judgment. That means they have either misappropriated, or mismanaged their money or missed God in a period of sowing when He told them to give. They are looking for their harvest, and it is not there.

Sometimes we pray, "Lord, I need $500.00 for this telephone bill," and God sends the $500.00. The light bill comes due and it is $450.00. If you take the $500.00 God sent for the telephone bill to pay the light bill, you will have a hard time getting the money to pay for that telephone bill, because the provision already came for it. You must use funds for the particular purpose for which they are sanctified. If you use it for another purpose, you misappropriate funds that God channeled in your direction.

I am really teaching you prophetically. God is giving you some prescriptions, so take them, and ingest them. They will work for you, but if you put them on the shelf, you will have to work your own way through that challenge.

I do not loan money to an individual unless I can forget about it. That is the principle of the Kingdom. If I give you money, then I'll say, "Take this. Don't pay me back." But if I loan you money, that changes our relationship, because the Bible says the borrower is servant to the lender (Proverbs 22:7). So if we have a friendship and I loan you money, that changes our relationship. It changes our friendship from friend and friend to servant and master.

When you borrow, it denotes that you are under judgment—not that you are in sin, but you *are* under judgment. You have missed God somewhere along the line. You have missed a direction or you took a wrong turn. These principles are designed to transform your life...to get your thinking straight. Learn to discern the difference between good and God, because everything that is good is not necessarily God. You can eat of the tree of the knowledge of good and evil, but it will still produce death. That's why you have to eat of the tree of life. You must discern the difference between good and God, because you can be doing something good, but still produce death.

I let people know, "The church is not a banking or loan institution." Some people say, "We should be able to come to the church and get a handout", but that is not what it is all about.

Beloved, we need to make sure that in our sowing we are not just moving in something that is good works and miss moving in God.

One time the Lord spoke and told me to fly to Pittsburgh to give a particular man of God $300.00. I didn't know why my wife and I were doing it, except that I knew God has spoken. We flew there together. It was an expensive trip, but we went out of obedience. We gave the envelope to the man as we were leaving to return home. He said, "You had no way of knowing this, but I was $300.00 short from closing on my home."

If I had missed this period of sowing, when the day came that I needed something at the last minute, it might not have come.

Some of you argue with God and then testify, "The Lord told me to do such-and-such last week, and I didn't do it. I guess I'd better obey God today." It is dangerous to disobey God or to be negligent in responding to Him. The next time you need something at the last minute and God doesn't come through, recall the last time you did that to someone else.

We can say, "Lord, I know You told me to give that to him, but he doesn't need it." God never told you to go by looks! We seem to think that filling a need is the call of God, but that is not what it is about.

When the Queen of Sheba came to Solomon, she brought $3.5 million worth of goods. Solomon already had everything, but wealth begets wealth. The key is in obedience to God, responding to what He wants. Some of us become so need oriented that we miss God.

The reason why some people are not successful is they have no motivation. Many people start their own businesses because they are disgusted with where they are. This is not intended as a put-down, but if wives would stop propping up their husbands, it would force them to get in contact with God.

I have a wife and five children and I have the only income, so I can't afford to fool around and miss God.

If my wife was propping me up, then I could afford to miss God every now and then. I could fool around and pick up a lot of different hobbies. I'd have more to waste, because she would pick up the extra load.

But when you are the sole provider, you can't afford to miss God. You continually keep an open ear to God, because you want to make sure you are in the right place at the right time.

If God speaks to me today and says, "Be in Cuba tomorrow morning at 8:00," my bags are being packed. I don't care how I get there. If God says I have got to be there at 8:00, I can't afford to miss Him.

Let's look at one individual who invented something we enjoy today: Colonel Sanders. He was at the point of retirement, and when he realized he couldn't live off of his retirement check, he got in the kitchen and started frying chicken! If everything had been all right with the Colonel, we wouldn't be enjoying Kentucky Fried chicken today!

The Colonel was in a situation where he *had* to do something. Sometimes we need to be in a "do" or "die" situation. Some of us have been in Momma's nest too long. We need to be one of the eagles who is kicked out. The eagle gives you three times to try to fly. She scoops you up, takes you up, shows you the air, drops you and lets you go. The third time, if you do not learn how to flap those wings and get it together, you are history! A thought! A memory!

Some people have been bailed out too long. Some of us have bailed our children out far too long, and we need to let them hit bottom. Sometimes they can play stupid, but when they are out there in the real world and they realize we are not going to give them a handout, they will learn how to flap and get it together very quickly.

A man came to me one time and said, "My wife makes much more than I do, and we know someone should stay home, so I think I am going to be a house husband." I jumped all over that man. When I got through with him, he didn't DARE stay home!! The Divine mandate upon a man compels him to provide. The home is not a man's place of expression. The scripture says that *wives* are to be the keepers of the home. This is not a "chauvinistic" issue, but simply God's order. The essence of manhood is castrated when the order of God is defied.

Years ago when two people planned to get married, the man asked the father's permission for his daughter's hand in marriage. The father asked a line of questions. God cross-examined Adam and Eve to find out what was going on. When we violate a principle and don't allow that cross-examination to take place, if that man starts beating you upside the head, you have no recourse, because you were never released to begin with.

This is a principle of authority. A daughter isn't supposed to run home to her parents everytime she argues with her husband or vice–versa. Parents should send their children home and allow them to develop the necessary maturity to function in marriage. They should have no part in it. There is a place for parents to present proper input. That is why it must be done under the authority of the church. Then if there are challenges, the pastor can say, "I put you together. What is the problem? You are in covenant with God, and we saw you joined together."

We need to understand that the center of attention at the wedding is not the bride. It is the priest, because he is the one who is officiating the covenant. You have two families, one sitting on one side and one on the other side, with the bride coming down the middle separating, then bringing them together in the marriage union. Marriage is a covenant, not a social institution.

One thing that men looked for in considering cutting covenant was the answer to the question, "Is there a future in this outfit?" Some of you married and didn't see a future at all. The Bible says, *"Be ye not unequally yoked together with unbelievers..."* (II Corinthians 6:14). When you are unequally yoked, one will just be cruising along, while the other is doing all the work. It would be best for you to remain single until you find the mate who you are to be joined with for life.

Wives should challenge their husbands. I think most men love a challenge. The challenge should be, "If you want to marry me, the day we get married, I leave my job."

There should be an understanding. The wife should take the attitude, "Anything I do is going to be around the home." When a wife goes out to work eight hours a day, that means she is giving another man eight hours of loyalty that she could be giving to her husband and family. There has been so much looseness in marriage, because the job develops a relationship, a contact, a loyalty. Many times the employer demands more of her time than the husband could ever demand. He gets 40 hours a week from her that the husband will never have in a week, when those 40 hours could be used in building the home and nurturing the children.

I dare you to trust God. I dare any man to take his wife off of work and trust God. Watch God provide as you enforce the covenant. You will have a good report in a couple of years when she says, "I finally got a man. He was man enough to believe God...He trusted God."

This is a principle of the Kingdom of God. Now, we are not saying that the woman should throw away her skills. She can do things part time, but do them around the home.

She can write a Christian magazine for women across America or write books. She doesn't have to throw her skills away. She can do the husband's bookkeeping and balance the checkbook. She can be her husband's personal secretary, but her loyalty is to the husband - not to another man.

Children need to see the wife honoring the husband. If the wife does not respect her husband, the children will not respect him as a father. Children are not stupid. They know who is the head of the home. I was eight years old, and I knew who had the keys. When the woman moves into the place God has given her, she will be as a queen. She will reign. She will rule by the power of influence. She is almost like the neck that turns the head, but she does it through influence.

She moves in such godly wisdom, power, might, and love that she is able to make decisions, but she does it in such a way that the husband is built up as head of that home. There will be such unity that he will even think he made the decisions on his own!

Chapter 6
Meditation - Key to Mind Renewal

"My mouth shall speak of wisdom, and the meditation of my heart shall be of understanding."

- Psalms 49:3

In the Western world particularly, we have basically lost the art of meditation as God meant it to be. We have moved into meditation, but to a degree, we have moved out of logic. I believe meditation is being restored to the Church, because meditation is really the entire key to success.

Meditation means "to murmur." Whatever we are meditating upon in our heart will run parallel with the words of our mouth. Usually, whatever we speak is what we have been meditating upon.

We need to learn how to change our meditation to line up with the Word of God and to understand the purpose of divine imagery.

Many times people attribute this type of activity to the occult, but we are going to look at it from a scriptural perspective. We need to understand that before there can be a counterfeit, there must first be the genuine or the original.

There is only one spirit realm, and we need to discern what spirit individuals are being motivated by. This has hindered many individuals from moving out in the Spirit of God to the degree they should be, because they have not learned that before there can be a false, there must first be a truth. We could not have counterfeit money until we first had real money. Once you have experienced the genuine, then you can discern that which is false.

For a period of time in my life I was a bank teller. We were not taught how to discern counterfeit money. We learned how to discern the counterfeit by handling the real. This is also true in the operation and movement of the Holy Spirit.

Psalms 19:14 talks about the words of our mouth being in alignment with the Kingdom of God. *"Let the words of my mouth, and the meditation of my heart, be acceptable in thy sight, O Lord, my strength, and my redeemer."*

Whatever the heart meditates upon is what the mouth will speak, so when we learn how to meditate upon the Word of God, we will have no problem in our communication.

The Word of Faith movement was a genuine move of the Spirit of God. God raised up men to teach His people faith, to teach them how to speak (how to change the confession of their mouth), and they began to come forth with truths and principles about, "You can have what you say."

I believe God has shown us that there is a higher level, and it has to do with the meditation of the Word of God, the meditation of the heart.

Our mouth will speak whatever our heart meditates upon. Groups like Christian Science and the positive thinkers are far from the truth, because they don't meditate upon the Lordship of Jesus Christ. They do not meditate upon the Word of God.

It is not enough just to confess, "I am well. I am not sick. I am healed." We are to meditate upon the Word of God that speaks concerning health and healing. As we meditate upon these Scriptures, the words of our mouth will become aligned with the meditation of our heart.

The Greek word for meditation, according to Vine's An Expository Dictionary of New Testament Words, is MELETAO, which means "to care for."

Another word for meditation could be "worry." Worry is a form of meditation. The only problem is that normally when you worry, you are meditating upon the wrong thing. God wants to bring us into a place to "worry" about the Word. That's what I call it: "worrying the Word of God".

We try to figure out how we are going to pay bills, what we are going to do about a particular situation, and we keep dwelling on it. Sometimes we can go for a whole hour or two or even a whole day rolling something over and over in our spirit. Then we go to bed with it on our mind, and we end up dreaming about it.

That's what is called meditating day and night, but the problem is that we are meditating upon the wrong thing. We worry and worry, we dream about it, and we wake up in the middle of the night thinking about the same problem, because our mind can't find a solution to it. This type of meditation does not produce life.

Old Testament Examples of Meditation

Meditation was a practice among the men of the Old Testament. Let's look at a situation in Genesis 24 where Isaac's mother had just passed away.

"And they blessed Rebekah, and said unto her, Thou art our sister, be thou the mother of thousands of millions, and let thy seed possess the gate of those which hate them.

And Rebekah arose, and her damsels, and they rode upon the camels, and followed the man: and the servant took Rebekah, and went his way.

And Isaac came from the way of the well Lahai-
roi; for he dwelt in the south country.
And Isaac went out to meditate in the field at
the eventide: and he lifted up his eyes, and saw,
and, behold, the camels were coming.
And Rebekah lifted up her eyes, and when she
saw Isaac, she lighted off the camel."

- Verses 60-64

Verse 63 says Isaac went out to meditate. When he meditated, he went into a wide open place. I believe the Holy Spirit desires for us to move into all God has in store for us by coming out of the world of limitation and going into an unlimited realm.

To meditate in the Hebrew means **"to bend down in body and mind."** Isaac was really bringing the whole of his being (spirit, soul, and body) into a position of receiving from God.

Often, we mechanically pray with our mouths, but our minds are on what we are preparing for dinner. I don't want to get into an area of legalism, but for an individual to spend five or ten minutes of pure, unbroken, intimate fellowship with God is quite significant. Much of what we have labeled "prayer" is not prayer at all. We spend the first hour attempting to take ourselves beyond the natural into the realm of the spirit. In the initial stages of learning to pray in the spirit, our minds are occupied by many distractions. Personally, I have found that it takes

81

approximately an hour for me to get a good break-through in prayer.

The Holy Spirit wants to bring us to a place where there is an emptying out of self. It is only when we are in that dimension that we are able to pray super-naturally and prophetically. We begin to reach over into the area of the unlimited. In that dimension of selflessness, we are able to pray supernaturally and prophetically as we reach into the realm of the unlimited.

In the dimension of prayer, where I command my soul to be still before God, the Holy Spirit takes me totally across international date lines. When I am praying, it is almost as if I am there. God wants to bring us into the realm of the spirit, an ongoing realm of eternity where there is no time or distance.

In the spirit you can simultaneously sense the past, present, and future. You can prophesy to someone, "Ten years ago the Lord did such and such a thing in your life. About five years ago, this began to happen." Then, in the same glance, you see something taking place about twenty years down the road.

You will see all three dimensions of time merging in one sphere, and it is the same way in prayer. The Holy Spirit wants to bring us to where we have a knowing of past, present, and future, because in God, there is no time. When you move at the speed of light, you supersede time. God is light.

The difference between dreaming and meditating is that one is aimless, while the other is thought tending to a particular object. I like the way a certain author put it. He said, "Prayer is the thought expressed, while meditation is the nurse of prayer." Prayer is the expression of those thoughts that are on the inside of us, but meditation is the real foundation of prayer, because your mouth will only speak that which your heart is meditating upon.

In every major move and visitation of God, He does a work of sovereignty and grace. Many believers are in a holding pattern, waiting for a sovereign visitation of God. That is good, because God will do a sovereign work. God is also moving to a place where we will not wait for a sovereign visitation, but the Holy Spirit is saying, "If you will, then I will." We are to recognize that we are not working for God; we are working with Him; we are co-laborers with Him.

Mark 16:20 says of the apostles, "*And they went forth, and preached every where, the Lord working with them, and confirming the word with signs following. Amen.*" The apostles understood a place of no limitation, and that is where the Father wants to bring us.

God will not confirm one's ministry, but He will confirm one's calling. He will confirm the Word that is spoken. That's how we begin to learn about giving in the supernatural. It is not the amount we give that God blesses, but it is the act of obedience. God always confirms and blesses obedience.

Scripture says the wheat and tares grow together, and God will do the separating. I believe just as there is to be a maturing of the sons of God, there is also to be a maturing of the sons of Satan. I believe we will see modern day reenactments of the prophets of Baal and the prophets of Elijah meeting face to face. Again, we will see Pharaoh's magicians challenging Moses' in face to face confrontations. In preparation for this day, I believe God will raise up schools of prophets across the country and around the world to teach people how to move in the supernatural, not just speaking of a God of miracles, but seeing the God of miracles in demonstration.

Meditation is a very important aspect of moving and demonstrating in the Holy Spirit.

> *"This book of the law shall not depart out of thy mouth; but thou shalt meditate therein day and night, that thou mayest observe to do according to all that is written therein: for then thou shalt make thy way prosperous, and then thou shalt have good success."*

> - Joshua 1:8

The law of God cannot depart out of anyone's mouth, except they meditate day and night. Again, meditate means **"to murmur or mutter to oneself over and over."** It is like talking to yourself.

An example of meditation is one saying, "Let me see what I am going to do about this...what I am going to do about that...I know I must take care of this and take care of that."

To ready ourselves for situations that may arise, we need to meditate and thank God that He is love. "I walk in love. Love never fails. Love seeks not its own."

Then when the enemy tries to attack us in an area, we need to meditate in the Word of God by murmuring to ourselves and allow the Word to manifest.

It is not enough to meditate upon the Word or memorize the Word if the corresponding action is not there. Without the "doing" of the Word, there will be confusion and the body will be out of alignment.

Remember, Isaac was able to bend down his spirit, body, and mind - the whole person. Paul refers to "the whole person" in I Thessalonians 5:23. *"And the very God of peace sanctify you wholly; and I pray God your whole spirit and soul and body be preserved blameless unto the coming of our Lord Jesus Christ."*

Sanctification is not denoted by clothing or what you look like outwardly. It means "a setting apart" My shoes has been sanctified for my feet, and they have both been sanctified to walk. I do not put shoes on my hands, neither do I try to walk with my hands. I can do some walking with my hands, but it would be strenuous since they have not been sanctified for that purpose.

The Lord wants to bring about the sanctification

and the preservation of the whole man - spirit, soul, and body. By the Spirit, we will move into new dimensions when we move into meditation where we bring the whole man into alignment.

Most cults tap into meditation, through soulish power. They never tap into the Lordship of Jesus Christ. It is without the motivation of the Holy Spirit, and it is void of God. Therefore, their manifestations are demonic.

The Bible give us the key to discerning the origin of the manifestation in I Corinthians 12:3, "..*no man speaking by the Spirit of God calleth Jesus accursed: and that no man can say that Jesus is Lord, but by the Holy Ghost.*" The Bible says that the testimony of Jesus is the spirit of prophecy. If a prophecy is not advancing the Kingdom of God and giving glory and honor to the Lordship of Jesus Christ, then we know it is contrary to God's Word and purposes.

The meditation of your heart will determine the success of your outer man.

According to Joshua, prosperity doesn't come by giving alone. Prosperity and success will come in two ways:

1. Meditating upon God's Word day and night.

2. "Doing" (or obeying) all of the Word.

In meditating God's way, He will prompt a thought or a scripture in your mind, and you will start to mutter or meditate upon it. Then the Holy Spirit will

86

bring illumination, light, truth, and revelation to that thought or scripture, and that is the thing He will cause your spirit to feed upon.

The Apostle John was speaking of meditation when he said, *"Beloved, I wish above all things that thou mayest prosper and be in health, even as thy soul prospereth"* (III John 2).

Your prosperity and health will spring forth in proportion to the time you spend in meditating upon God's Word. The status of your prosperity and health depends upon the renewal of the inner man rather than the outer man.

You may hear people referring to these principles while discussing metaphysics or transcendental meditation, but remember: you can get a monkey to plug in a light! But we must learn how to discern the difference between working the principles of God and knowing the God of the principles! God wants to bring us to the place that we might know Him. Paul said to the church at Philippi, "That I may know Him..." That word "know" is the same word that is used when Scripture says that Adam knew Eve. They are talking about coming into intimate relationship with Him.

> *That I may know him, and the power of his resurrection, and the fellowship of his sufferings, being made conformable unto his death.*
>
> - Philippians 3:10

87

We can learn the principles of prosperity, healing, and prayer, yet not know the God of all these things. Meditation is really meditating upon a person, the Lord Jesus Christ, causing the Word to become flesh.

In David we find another Old Testament example of meditation. He said, *"Give ear to my words, O Lord, consider my meditation"* (Psalms 5:1).

Music plays an important role in meditation. It helps to calm and strengthen the inner man. It is imperative that the music used to meditate upon underscores and echoes the Word of God. Music that carries a contrary message will negate the influence of your conscious study of Scripture. Music contains an innate power to establish its rhythym or pattern in your mind. Did you ever have a song affect your sub-conscious to such a degree that you find yourself involuntarily singing it? Godly music will engraft itself in your spirit and cause you to grow in the knowledge of the Lord. Satanic or soulish music is not able to plant life in your heart, but becomes a malevolent force to detract from your life by planting ungodly seeds for your sub-conscious to meditate upon. Occasionally, a person's soul is disquieted by outside pressures and dilemmas that interrupt their focus upon God. The prophet Elijah found it necessary to call for a ministrel when he was being asked to prophesy the word of the Lord. Music assists in quieting the soul to hear the Voice of God.

Meditation Among the Ungodly

Meditation is a common practice among the ungodly. Isaiah speaks of it.

> *"For your hands are defiled with blood, and your fingers with iniquity; your lips have spoken lies, your tongue hath muttered [meditated] perverseness.*
>
> *In transgressing and lying against the Lord, and departing away from our God, speaking oppression and revolt, conceiving and uttering from the heart words of falsehood."*

> - Isaiah 59:3, 13

Isaiah's inditement against this ungoldly clan centers around what was conceived in their hearts through meditation, then spoken by their lips. You will speak whatever your heart meditates upon. You will prophesy what your heart meditates upon. You can prophesy according to the proportion of your faith. The extent of a prophetic word will be determined by the level of the Word of God that the person had dwelling on the inside of him. If there is little knowledge of God's Word, there will be a limited degree of His Word flowing forth. You can only give out whatever is within. If there is nothing within, then there will be nothing coming out.

Another form of meditation among the ungodly is described in Proverbs 24:1-2.

"Be not thou envious against evil men, neither desire to be with them.

For their heart studieth destruction, and their lips talk of mischief".

To "study destruction" is another form of meditation. If you have ever studied or crammed for an exam, you will have used this form. It is one thing to read the Word, but another thing to study it.

I can read the Bible from cover to cover, but it is another thing to meditate upon or study it from cover to cover. It will take a while, because you might stay in one verse an entire day. You might look it up in the Greek and the Hebrew. The Holy Spirit can bring such light in a word study, and you may find yourself spending hours in one Scripture.

God will have you continue to chew the cud. That's what meditation is.

Let's look at Psalm 2:1-2.

"Why do the heathen rage, and the people imagine a vain thing?
The Kings of the earth set themselves, and the rulers take counsel together, against the Lord, and against his anointed..."

The word imagine is the same word for meditate. In other words, "Why do the people imagine (or meditate) a vain thing?" Our imagination is to be submitted unto God so that His Image can be seen in every area of life.

Test of Meditation - Obedience

We test the value, degree, or level of meditation by

the obedience which results. If our meditations are upon God and His Word, they will produce life. If we are not meditating upon God's Word, our meditations will produce death.

There were two trees in the Garden of Eden: the tree of life and the tree of the knowledge of good and evil. We must make a decision between good and God. We can eat of the tree of the knowledge of good, but it will still produce death if it is not God.

Buddhism has a lot of good philosophical theory within it, but it still produces death, because moral goodnesss will not produce eternal life. So there is a distinct difference between good and God.

God wants us to eat of the tree of life by whatever we meditate upon. And if it is not God, it will not produce life. Instead, it will produce death, which means separation from God or alienation from life.

Chapter 7
Quieting of the Soul to Move into the Deep

"As the hart panteth after the water brooks, so panteth my soul after thee, O God.

My soul thirsteth for God, for the living God: when shall I come and appear before God?

My tears have been my meat day and night, while they continually say unto me, Where is thy God?

When I remember these things, I pour out my soul in me: for I had gone with the multitude, I went with them to the house of God, with the voice of joy and praise, with a multitude that kept holyday.

Why art thou cast down, O my soul? and why art thou disquieted in me? hope thou in God: for I shall yet praise him for the help of his countenance.

O my God, my soul is cast down within me: therefore will I remember thee from the land of Jordan, and of the Hermonites, from the hill Mizar. Deep calleth unto deep..."

- Psalm 42:1-7

Meditation will teach us how to reach into the depths of our spirits and go into areas where we have never been before to connect with God. There are varying levels and degrees to the glory and manifestations of the Spirit. God deals with every man at his level of knowledge of His Word. Remember when Jesus was with His disciples, He said, *"I have yet many things to say unto you, but ye cannot bear them now"* (John 16:12).

God will deal with each one of us differently. There are degrees to His glory and to His dealing. God never dealt with Moses by way of the burning bush. When the children of Israel were to go up to hear God speak, they found God dealing with Moses in a depth (or realm) that they were not familiar with. They basically said, "Never mind, Moses. You go in and hear God for us, and we will stay here."

Yet, there was another degree of glory that God used to deal with the children of Israel and that was the cloud by day and the pillar of fire by night.

94

Jesus had great manifestations of glory in His earthly ministry. When Jesus said, **"I AM,"** the soldiers fell backwards. When God came unto the prophets, they were overcome with the awesomeness of His Presence.

In Scripture, when someone fell under the power of God, the individual was usually under judgment. Now, judgment is not a negative thing.

When a person is hospitalized in intensive care, we understood, "The individual is critical." Often, we think that's a negative statement, but "critical" simply means they are at a turning point. They will either turn for the better or for the worse. It is a time of reckoning, for their condition has now come to a point where whichever way they turn, that's it. Either they will come right out of this thing, or they will be eliminated.

I personally believe that the Church is in critical condition because the Holy Spirit wants to bring us to a place where we can contain that eternal weight of glory when His anointing comes upon us. He wants us to learn how to soak it in and receive it. Now, there will be those times when we can't contain it, because we will perceive the awesomeness of His glory.

I remember when I first came to the Lord. No one taught me how or when to fall out under the anointing of God. The Spirit of God was so awesome, I couldn't stand, because I couldn't contain it. If Adam was still walking in the image of God, wearing that eternal weight of glory the Father gave him, when the time of fellowship came, Adam would not have been consumed, because he was in the image and likeness of God.

I Thessalonians 5:17 says, *"Pray without ceasing."* Our lives must become a prayer. We must learn to practice God's Presence and walk in the Spirit all the time, whether at work or in prayer. That is how we increase our depth of fellowship with God.

God usually creates, places, and deals with His precious things (the value of gold) in the deep. Diamonds are made under pressure. Oysters or pearls are formed under pressure. They dwell under the deep. There are truths or gems in the realm of the Spirit, where we learn how to go into the depths of what the Lord is speaking.

Often, it becomes difficult to communicate these truths. Paul said when he was caught up into the heavens, he heard things that were unlawful for him to utter. I believe Paul could not find words in the natural to explain that which he saw in the Spirit.

I believe there is more depth to the art of communication. If God shows you a 15-year span and you have to communicate that to a body of believers, you will have to find the words. That's why there are different levels of prophecy.

God speaks to us, not in words, but in pictures. I could say dog, and each person would get a mental picture of a dog. You didn't see D-O-G. Perhaps you saw a picture of your own dog, a neighbor's dog, or a picture of a dog on television. God uses imagery to communicate to us.

I could say house, and everyone would see something totally different. What we see is usually something the Holy Spirit is speaking to us. As we get a picture of house, some think of comfort, some about safety, others about security, and others about a house they want. As I shared this in a seminar, one person even thought of a house of government - the Senate.

If I were to say a black house, some would say, "I see a witch's castle...I see a house painted black...I see a house that has been devastated...I see a home filled with darkness." Usually, we don't think in words like "house," but we see an image of something when a word is spoken.

When the Holy Spirit speaks to us, He speaks in images, and He deals with us according to our knowledge. For example, an individual might say, "I don't know what this means, but I see a river running up and down the wall." We get in trouble when we try to interpret. If the Holy Spirit tells us to tell an individual to see a river up and down the road, deliver the message, but leave the interpretation alone.

The person might respond, "I understand what it means," yet you can't discern any meaning whatsoever!

Can you imagine how the prophets felt when they prophesied, "Unto us a child is born. Unto us a Son is given. A virgin is going to have a child." They must have been looked upon as some of the craziest people in Israel!

We get in big trouble when we try to interpret and apply instead of just delivering what the Father gives us.

We need to leave the communing and sharing of the revelation to the Holy Spirit. We interrupt God's communication process when we try to explain His dealings.

Watching And Praying

Jesus talks about watching and praying. *"Take ye heed, watch and pray: for ye know not when the time is"* (Mark 13:33). Watch and pray are the key words in this verse. It is not enough just to pray. We must "watch and pray".

In this verse, Jesus is speaking of the coming of the Lord. We are not just to pray, but we are also to watch. We are to be looking for Him.

God wants to teach us how to watch for the spiritual comings of the Lord. There are many comings. I believe there was a coming of the Lord with Martin Luther: a coming of the nearness of the Presence of God restoring truth back to the Body of Christ. There was a coming of the Presence of the Lord with John Wesley, bringing sanctification back into the church. There was a coming of the Presence of the Lord in the Azusa Street Revival of 1906.

There was a coming of the Lord in 1948 with the Latter Rain movement. Then there was a coming with the Healing revival that came forth in the '50s. In the '60s, God began to do something supernatural in church growth and in raising up supernatural pastors, men after God's own heart, to build churches for the Kingdom of God. Then, I believe 1988 was the beginning of another visitation.

Some individuals thought the Lord was coming in 1988. In looking at the Scriptures, I believe in the eminent return of the Lord, but I also believe that we will see the restitution of all things. There is to be a watching, but I believe the Body of Christ is sensing another visitation from the throne of God.

In the '70s, people were looking for the coming of the Lord. They went out on beaches waiting for God, and I believe what they were really sensing was another move of God. God brought the word of faith move during that time. I believe the word of faith move came because the charismatic renewal moved into all Spirit and no Word. People were prophesying in the name of Mary and all types of weird things, so God had to bring truth, teaching and doctrine back into the Church.

Let's go to Habakkuk 2:1. *"I will stand upon my watch, and set me upon the tower, and will watch to see what he will say unto me, and what I shall answer when I am reproved."*

When he talks about, "I will stand upon my watch," this is a call to watchmen. Every prophet in the Body of Christ is called to move into a realm of a seer or a watchman.

> *"And the Lord answered me, and said, Write the vision, and make it plain upon tables, that he may run that readeth it.*
>
> *For the vision is yet for an appointed time, but at the end it shall speak, and not lie: though it tarry, wait for it; because it will surely come, it will not tarry"*

(Habakkuk 2:2-3).

The vision must be written down. Those of us who are watchmen must learn how to get into the area of writing. Just as there were writing prophets in the Old Testament, God wants to develop writing prophets for today.

I recently read of a man who says another way of practicing God's Presence is that we write down everything we sense God is speaking to us. As we get into the writing aspect, we understand with more clarity. We learn how to discern that which is the voice of the Lord and that which is not.

I encourage people to keep a personal diary and write down the thought the Father gives them for each day. You might be surprised how those things will minister to you when you refer to them. You will find that there has been a leadership of the Spirit all along. We are going to write down all the different prophecies God has spoken to the Body of Christ at our local church, Zoe. They may not have much value now, but they will later in their season of manifestation. It has meaning now, but it will have more meaning later when someone picks up the prophecy of 30 years ago and says, "This is what God was speaking." We are commanded to write the vision down.

When we begin to practice the Presence of God, we will realize that the soul must be quieted. In Psalm 42:5, David says, *"Why art thou cast down, O my soul? and why art thou disquieted in me? hope thou in God: for I shall yet praise him for the help of his countenance."* When we understand the importance of quieting our soul in God's Presence, we will learn how to receive from Him. The soul must be brought under the authority of the Spirit for true meditation to take place. If your soul is superceding that which is of the Spirit, then it will not produce the degree of light that God would expect it to produce. Many people are moving in soulish power and energy. God doesn't want us to move by the power of the soul. He wants us to move by the power of His Spirit. Paul said in I Thessalonians 4:11, *"And that ye study to be quiet, and to do your own business, and to work with our own hands, as we commanded you."* The soul must be quieted in order to hear.

"To be quiet" doesn't mean you need to go find a room where no one is talking. It means the quieting of the inner man. I could be in a room with thousands of people and instantly quiet my soul to be able to say, "Lord, I need to hear what You are saying." I don't need to say, "I need to go and pray, excuse me for about 20 minutes. Then I will return with a clearer word." We must learn to quiet our soul. The conflict people get into is not that they can't prophesy or deliver a word. The problem is they don't know how to quiet their soul. All types of thoughts start to bombard your soul, and all types of fears try to creep up. "What if it is wrong? What if it isn't God? Suppose it is the devil telling me this? Suppose I mess up this individual's life?"

These types of thoughts keep the soul disturbed to the point we are not able to bless anyone. Our soul is not quieted. Formally, I attended in a church where I went through battles like that. Some of the thoughts that bombarded me were, "Suppose they tell me to shut up. Suppose they tell me to sit down. Suppose they embarrass me." You can go through an argument like that for a good half hour and become so weary. I had to break through that. I had to quiet my soul and command my mind, "Why are you so disquieted? Be thou quiet, O soul." After that, I sensed the prompting of the Father to prophesy, and I stood and delivered the word of the Lord.

We are not talking about churches of 100 people. A couple of times I went to big conferences at Madison Square Garden and prophesied. They didn't know me, and I didn't know them, but I stood up and prophesied at the direction of the Lord. My soul went through a multiplicity of changes, but I had to quiet my soul.

My entire being was bombarded with thoughts like, "Suppose they don't hear you and start talking over you. You are going to make the biggest fool of yourself! Suppose they tell you to shut up in front of all these 5,000 people. Then what are you going to do?" If we are going to be vessels through which the Spirit of God flows, we must learn how to quiet the soul.

Exploring New Dimensions of God

I Corinthians 14:4 says, *"He that speaketh in an unknown tongue edifieth himself; but he that prophesieth edifieth the church."*

Another area of meditation is praying in tongues. Whenever we speak in tongues, we build ourselves up. While we are praying in the Spirit, we will also be praying in our understanding. *"For he that speaketh in an unknown tongue speaketh not unto men, but unto God: for no man understandeth him; howbeit in the spirit he speaketh mysteries"* (I Corinthians 14:2).

Let me crush another sacred cow. There is no such thing as a message in tongues. He that speaks in an unknown tongue speaks unto God. So whenever you are speaking in tongues, you are not speaking to men, but you are speaking to God. Tongues and interpretation are not equivalent to prophecy. It is not the

103

same thing. Why would God take you through the changes of speaking in tongues when you could speak out directly?

Follow after charity, and desire spiritual gifts,
but rather that ye may prophesy.

- I Corinthians 14:1

Much of what we call the interpretation of tongues is not the interpretation of tongues at all. Tongues, I believe, is the New Testament ministry of psalming unto the Lord. It is like when David spoke what was in his heart unto God. When I am speaking in tongues, I am talking to the Father.

When someone prays in tongues and another person gives an interpretation of what the person prayed in the Spirit, we can have a sensing that God is saying something. We are not saying that the prophecy is wrong. I believe we are going to see pure interpretation where an individual speaks out of his spirit and cries unto God, "My soul will follow hard after thee, O God. Early in the morning I will rise up and seek thee. We thank You for gracing us with Your Presence in this place today. How we magnify You and love Thy Name, for Thou art a great God, and Thou art highly exalted and forever to be praised. Amen." That would be an interpretation of a tongue of that which I spoke to the Spirit out of my spirit.

"What is it then? I will pray with the spirit, and
I will pray with the understanding also: I will

104

sing with the spirit,and I will sing with the understanding also.

Else when thou shalt bless with the spirit (that is speaking in tongues), how shall he that occupieth the room of the unlearned say Amen at thy giving of thanks, seeing he understandeth not what thou sayest?"

- Verses 15-16

Notice, they were giving a message, but it was a giving of thanks. In Acts, chapter 2, when they spoke in tongues, they, too, were magnifying God.

"Wherefore let him that speaketh in an unknown tongue pray that he may interpret."

- I Corinthians 14:13

I believe any individual who speaks in tongues has the ability to interpret that which he speaks. God does not give a calling without equipping with all that is needed for that call. If there is no interpreter, you are to pray that you may interpret. God would not tell you to pray for something that He wouldn't give you or that you wouldn't be able to receive.

"For if I pray in an unknown tongue, my spirit prayeth, but my understanding is unfruitful".

- I Corinthians 14:14

When we pray in an unknown tongue, our spirit prays. It is coming out of our inner man, and our mind (our understanding) in unfruitful.

105

Stages of Meditation

There are stages of coming into a place of prayer or meditation. We usually initiate it from the external realm. We begin to think about what we did today, how long it took us to get here, how long it is going to take us to get back home, and what we are going to eat for dinner. That's the external realm.

Then we speak of things we feel in the natural. "I was very aggravated, Lord. I am going through this, and I am going through that. I am frustrated in this area. When are You going to do the miracle on my job I have been asking for? When are You going to do the things in my finances I have been looking for You to do?"

Then you begin to speak of the dreams that are in your inner man. "Lord, You know I really desire to move over there. I desire that home over there. I desire to do this for You, Lord, if You will provide this."

You start to dream. You speak of the dreams that are in your heart. Then you begin to sit quietly in His Presence and hear only Jesus. That is when you come to the area of quieting your soul, where you say, "I am only going to hear what You have to say, Lord. I don't want to hear anything but You."

Jesus lived a whole life of divine imagery. He said, "I only do that which I see the Father doing." The Lord wants each of us to come to this point. We are to quiet the soul where we only do that which we see the Father doing.

What do we see the Father doing with a deaf child? We see the Father open his ears, and we get in agreement. We do only that which we see the Father do. We end up becoming the Word made flesh, making that Word the image that God is speaking. We begin to bring prophecy out of the supernatural and bring it into the natural.

We become like that which we meditate upon. Whatever we worship is what we will become. Likewise, in meditation, the things that we meditate upon are the things that we become. There is an old saying that we are whatever we eat. That is true with our minds, too. Whatever we feed our mind is what we will become. If we feed on worldly magazines, that is what we will become. If we feed on soap operas, that is what our lives will become. We will convey the same worldly principles in our lifestyles.

As we learn to quiet the soul, we will move into deeper realms of the Spirit.

Quieting Of The Soul To Move Into The Deep

Chapter 8
The Fruit of Meditation

"Blessed is the man that walketh not in the counsel of the ungodly, nor standeth in the way of sinners, nor sitteth in the seat of the scornful.

But his delight is in the law of the Lord; and in his law doth he meditate day and night.

And he shall be like a tree planted by the rivers of water, that bringeth forth his fruit in his season; his leaf also shall not wither; and whatsoever he doeth shall prosper.

The ungodly are not so: but are like the chaff which the wind driveth away.

Therefore the ungodly shall not stand in the judgment, nor sinners in the congregation of the righteous.

The Fruit Of Meditation

For the Lord knoweth the way of the righteous:
but the way of the ungodly shall perish".

- Psalms 1

Psalms 1 gives us a pattern for meditation: there must be a delighting in the law of the Lord. A person who delights himself in the law of the Lord will not walk in the counsel of the ungodly; he will have no part in the actions of sinners; and he will have no fellowship with those who scorn.

Psalms 1 also shows us the fruit of meditation. Meditation causes a person to delight in the law of the Lord, and delighting in the law brings great satisfaction. In fact, meditation in God's law will build character. The person who meditates day and night in God's law is compared to a flourishing tree, for meditation brings prosperity.

"And he shall be like a tree planted by the rivers
of water, that bringeth forth his fruit in his sea-
son; his leaf also shall not wither; and whatsoever
he doeth shall prosper".

- Verse 3

Meditation is the art of engrafting. Trees are often engrafted. You can slice a tree, engraft a branch, and cause that new branch to grow. The same principle is true with the Word of God.

Engrafting is accomplished by slicing a branch from one tree to another. The branch will retain its own distinct fruit while receiving nourishment from the

110

tree into which it was engrafted. James speaks to the Church when he says, *"Wherefore lay apart all filthiness and superfluity of naughtiness, and receive with meekness the engrafted word which is able to save your souls"* (James 1:21).

There is a difference in being born-again of the Spirit and the salvation of the soul. Sinners are born-again in their spirit, but their souls are still unsaved. The salvation of the soul comes forth with the engrafting of the Word of God. James says, *"...receive with meekness the engrafted word, which is able to save your souls* [or preserve your soul].

Soul salvation takes place when there is teaching of the Word. On Sunday mornings I am saving souls. I am preserving souls by feeding them with the Word that is able to keep them.

If the truth of the Word has been engrafted in a soul properly, it will set a seal in that area, and that part of the individual's soul is saved.

As we engraft portions of Scripture into our soul and nourish it through meditation, the Word will ultimately produce the rich spiritual fruit of what is expressed in that portion of Scripture. For example, if we have a challenge with love, we should meditate upon I Corinthians 13.

Many people in the Word of Faith movement meditated continually on prosperity Scriptures. They walked in prosperity, because that area of their soul

111

was saved. They engrafted that Word on the inside of them until it became a part of them...until they became that Word made flesh or the Word made visible. They demonstrated the prosperity of God.

You are what you eat! Another terminology that I like is that you are a product of your confession. This is why we are to teach and admonish one another in psalms and hymns and spiritual songs (Colossians 3:16).

God will cause His Word to be engrafted into people through songs. Have you ever had a tune in your heart and it stayed with you all day? That song was being engrafted into your soul. This is why we need more songs that are Scripturally oriented. The Word that is constantly sung will become a natural expression of our lives. Our lives will begin to express the Word.

We are to be like trees planted by rivers of water. We are to understand our seasons. Just because an apple tree does not bear fruit in the winter doesn't mean it is not an apple tree. Some people are going through a season where it is not quite time for their fruit to come forth. You will bear the fruit in your due season, in the season that God has ordained for it to come forth, but not until then. We need to learn divine timing in meditation.

The secret of meditation is that your joy is in the law of the Lord. His Word will be upon your mind day and night. As you look at your life compared to the life of a tree, you will understand that the source of your life comes from God.

Note, also, that a tree is planted, not self sown. We are to be "planted of the Lord" in a local church, rather than to sow or plant ourselves. If we are planted by the Lord, then God will do some unusual things. We will see the divine connection that God brings about when we understand the purpose of planting.   Meditation causes our roots, as that of a tree, to reach down very deep so we can draw from the water that is near. We need to learn how to reach down deep so we can draw from the rivers of the Spirit of life.

The Fruit Of Meditation

Chapter 9
Practicing Meditation

The three basic things involved in practicing meditation are:

1. Reading the Scriptures;

2. Praying the Scriptures; and

3. Hearing the Voice of the Lord.

Paul said, *"Till I come, give attendance to reading, to exhortation, to doctrine"* (I Timothy 4:13).

When you come together, make sure that you come together for reading, exhortation, and doctrine. You are to think upon the things that have been spoken over you in prophecy, and do not forget when hands were laid on you by the presbytery. Do not take those things lightly. Meditate on, roll that thing over, allow it to become a part of you, begin to embrace it, and walk in it. However, you must not neglect it.

Reading differs from study. *"Study to shew thyself approved unto God, a workman that needeth not to be ashamed, rightly dividing the word of truth"* (II Timothy 2:15).

The message in this verse is "to be diligent." God wants us to be diligent in the area of seeking His approval. When they read the law, no revelation followed. The Holy Spirit wants to bring revelation, illumination, clarification, and meditation. It is not enough just to read the law. God wants us to look beyond the letter and get to the Spirit of the Word. Remember, the letter kills, but the Spirit gives life. So we must move beyond the letter and into the dimension of the Spirit and begin to pray the Scriptures. However, before praying the Scriptures, we must always acknowledge God. If we don't first acknowledge God, we could move into a lot of soulish activity. Proverbs 3:6 says, *"In all thy ways acknowledge him, and he shall direct thy paths."*

Then we are to commit our works unto the Lord. *"Commit thy works unto the Lord, and thy thoughts shall be established"* (Proverbs 16:3).

Science has shown us that there are two areas of the brain: a right hemisphere where we move in the area of creativity, and a left hemisphere which is the realm of logic. I have often wondered why, seemingly, there are more women than men prophesying and moving in the things of the Spirit. Sometimes, it is because of the woman's nature. The woman is usually very intuitive and sensitive, and she operates from the area of the right hemisphere of her brain. Those operating from the left hemisphere operate in the realm of logic. Often, they reason themselves right out of the moving of the Spirit.

A person moving in the area of logic might say, "It doesn't make sense, God. I can't do it unless You send me ten confirmations, and each one must be spelled out exactly like this." A person moving in logic limits God and allows the shackles of reason to stunt their growth in the miracle working power of God.

The prophetic realm operates by the Spirit, but God will take the right hemisphere of a person's mind and open up the arena of His creativity.

Paul says, *"Neglect not the gift that is in thee, which was given thee by prophecy, with the laying on of the hands of the presbytery"* (Verse 14).

By prophecy and the laying on of hands, there is an impartation. There should never be a departation until there is an impartation. This is a principle of the Spirit. There was no departing until there was an imparting.

Before Moses departed, he imparted into Joshua. Before Aaron departed, he imparted into Eleazar. Before Elijah departed, he imparted into Elisha. Jesus did not depart until He imparted into His disciples.

117

The true value of the School of Prophets is that people are being discipled. Some people have problems with discipleship, because their souls have not been renewed in this area of authority.

When Samuel, the head of the School of the Prophets, was called by God, he said, "Eli, is that you?" Did you ever wonder why Samuel thought it was Eli's voice? I believe it's because when God speaks, He sounds like those He has delegated to be in authority over us.

When Elijah was getting ready to depart, everyone being discipled under him knew something was about to happen.

I believe the prophets that God sets in the local body are to be close to the shepherd to be discipled, because every prophet needs to sit under a strong leader to help tutor them. I believe we have missed the importance of the ministry of the mentor.

In some cases, our churches have begun to resemble our education system where we fill people with a bunch of information, but neglect to give them an opportunity to experience the application of the information.

In the school of prophets, they were not just taught the theory of the prophetic mode, but they moved in demonstration and the word of the Lord. Samuel stood as a senior prophet, and he orchestrated the entire move of the Spirit. God does not flow unless there is structure and order. There must always be a senior head. Even in a plurality of leadership, there must always be a senior man in authority who God will speak to in the area of emphasis.

When Barnabas and Paul were together, there was a senior man. It started off as Barnabas and Paul, and then it switched to Paul and Barnabas.

Hearing the Voice of the Lord

God is always speaking. He is simply waiting for us to tune in! We saw in Revelation 2:11, the word to the Church, *"He that hath an ear, let him hear what the Spirit saith unto the churches..."* Exodus 33:20 says *"...thou canst not see my face: for there shall no man see me, and live."*

In Madame Guyon's book, Experiencing the Depths of Jesus Christ, she says, "If your prayer still contains your own life, then that prayer cannot see God, for no man can see God and live." The prayer that you pray must be the prayer that is on the heart of the Father (that is the will of the Father), or that prayer will not be able to live. It must be your made-alive spirit bearing witness with the Spirit of God or it cannot live.

Prayer that proceeds from your mind is only the beginning, but union with Christ is the end. This same principle is applicable with meditation.

We start from the external realm, but the end is that we will become that which we have meditated upon. We are to become like Jesus and mirror His image.

Chapter 10
Logos and Rhema Words

To fully comprehend the concept of meditation, we need to understand the difference between "logos" and "rhema."

Logos

Logos denotes the expression of thought, not the mere name of an object, as embodying a conception or idea. Logos also is the personal Word, a title of the Son of God, as we see in the book of John.

> *"In the beginning was the Word, and the Word was with God, and the Word was God.*
> *The same was in the beginning with God.*
> *All things were made by him; and without him was not any thing made that was made".*

> - John 1:1-3

All things were made by Jesus, who is the Word. This verse shows His creative power.

Verse 4 reads, *"In him was life; and the life was the light of men."*

The logos can also be looked at as the written Word of God.

> *"And the Word was made flesh, and dwelt among us, (and we beheld his glory, the glory as of the only begotten of the Father,) full of grace and truth."*
>
> — Verse 14

Notice the message the angel brought to Mary in the account found in Luke, chapter one.

> *"And the angel said unto her, Fear not, Mary: for thou hast found favour with God.*
>
> *And, behold, thou shalt conceive in thy womb, and bring forth a son, and shalt call his name JESUS.*
>
> *He shall be great, and shall be called the Son of the Highest: and the Lord God shall give unto him the throne of his father David:*
>
> *And he shall reign over the house of Jacob for ever; and of his kingdom there shall be no end.*
>
> *Then said Mary unto the angel, How shall this be, seeing I know not a man?*
>
> *And the angel answered and said unto her, The Holy Ghost shall come upon thee, and the power of the Highest shall overshadow thee: therefore*

also that holy thing which shall be born of thee shall be called the Son of God.

And, behold, thy cousin Elisabeth, she hath also conceived a son in her old age: and this is the sixth month with her, who was called barren.

For with God nothing shall be impossible."

- Verses 30-37

In Verse 37, the word **"nothing"** in Greek actually says, *"No word of God is void of power."* The thing that caused Mary to conceive was the Word. The Word was made flesh and dwelt among her.

One Bible scholar said that the early church fathers celebrated during the time of the feast of lights, which would be in December—about the time we celebrate Christmas. They believed that was the time when the angel came unto Mary. It was the time of the conception. That was during the feast of lights. That is why Jesus can say, *"I am the light of the world."*

They believed that nine months later the Word was born, which was during the feast of tabernacles. That is why Scripture says, *"And the Word was made flesh..."*

This same principle is in effect when God speaks prophecy into your life. You are to meditate upon it, water it, and carry it until due season. However, you can miscarry a word.

Paul spoke of being *"...one born out of due time"* (I Corinthians 15:8).

It is possible to have a premature birth. People can

123

bring forth premature revelation. When Paul said that he was a man born out of due time, it actually means that he was born prematurely. We see later that Peter, who walked with Jesus, said that some of Paul's writings were hard to understand. [It is possible that some of Paul's revelation was premature].

It has been said that if you are one step ahead of the people and you become a leader. When you move two steps ahead, you become a martyr. If you don't believe this, try to discuss some of the information we have shared in this book with some of your acquaintances. We have talked about imagery and Jesus being led by a continual life of divine images. Your acquaintances will give you a look of bewilderment!

You might become a martyr in your fellowship. Then again, you might be tempted to go to the other extreme and become an individual who becomes a flake, real spooky and weird. That is not the Kingdom of God, because it is not the image of the Father. Jesus didn't walk around in a mystical manner. I believe there was a continual glory about Him.

Rhema

The word rhema denotes **"that which is spoken, what is uttered in speech or writing."**

The significance of rhema, as distinct from logos, is exemplified in the injunction to take *"...the sword of the Spirit, which is the word of God"* (Ephesians 6:17). This refers to the spoken Word of God [or rhema].

Paul tells us about the requirements of putting on the whole armor of God. In Verse 13, he says, *"Wherefore take upon you the whole armor of God..."*

To have on the whole armor of God, means you will be able to act and be just like God wants us to be. If we have the whole armor on, the devil won't know whether he is fighting against us or Jesus, because we have on His clothing! We are dressed in God's suit of armor.

When Adam was created in the image of God, he walked as an exact image or likeness of God. That's why all of creation was able to respond to Adam the way they were called to respond to him. He was able to name all of the creatures, because he was in the image of God. When he fell into sin, he fell short of that image. He walked in the image of something else.

We walk in the image of whatever kingdom we operate in. That is why the Bible says that rebellion is as the sin of witchcraft, because we are operating in a different kingdom when we operate in rebellion. We are operating in the Kingdom of this world where the modus operandi is witchcraft.

Let's examine the armor of God so we know how to dress appropriately each day.

> *"Wherefore, take unto you the whole armor of God, that ye may be able to withstand in the evil day, and having done all, to stand.*
> *Stand therefore, having your loins girt about*

with truth, and having on the breastplate of righteousness;

And your feet shod with the preparation of the gospel of peace;

Above all, taking the shield of faith, wherewith ye shall be able to quench all the fiery darts of the wicked.

And take the helmet of salvation, and the sword of the Spirit, which is the word of God".

- Ephesians 6:13-17

Paul is speaking of the rhema or spoken Word of God. Let's not wait for the enemy to come against us. Let's go out after the enemy. We are to go with a rhema [or spoken Word of God]. God wants to take us from the letter of the law to the spoken Word. A lot of people do things out of the letter instead of waiting for the rhema. You see, there is a time and then there is the fullness of time. Many times we birth things prematurely, and it doesn't have a chance to live because "the fullness of time" has not come.

Logos is the written Word of God, while rhema is God's Word spoken through our mouths to a specific situation.

Whenever we are meditating, we can meditate on the logos, but while meditating on the written Word, out of it will come a rhema [a specific word]. Let me give you an example. At the age of 19, the Lord told me to meditate on Isaiah 49:23.

"And kings shall be thy nursing fathers, and

*their queens thy nursing mothers: they shall bow
down to thee with their face toward the earth, and
lick up the dust of thy feet; and thou shalt know
that I am the Lord: for they shall not be ashamed
that wait for me".*

Everyday as I returned home on the subway, I meditated upon that verse. Out of this verse, God spoke to me: "You shall minister to leaders of nations. You shall minister to queens and kings".

I used to roll that over in my spirit, and wonder what God was saying. Then God began to send prophets to prophesy His purposes with further clarity. I wondered at the enormity of what God was saying.

Then, in 1983, I ministered to the prince and the queen of Swaziland, and later to other international government leaders. All of this came as a result of rhema that God spoke during a time of meditation.

This word was conceived in the womb of my spirit and flesh was given to it. Hallelujah!

Chapter 11

The Role of Meditation for the Prophet

Imagery is defined by Webster's dictionary as: *1) Images of objects taken collectively; statues; carved or sculptured figures; 2) Formation of mental images or the images thus formed.*

The Bible has something to say about false images in Exodus 20:4-5. Let's look at these verses.

> *"Thou shalt not make unto thee any graven image, or any likeness of any thing that is in heaven above, or that is in the earth beneath, or that is in the water under the earth:*
>
> *Thou shalt not bow down thyself to them, nor serve them: for I the Lord thy God am a jealous*

God, visiting the iniquity of the fathers upon the children unto the third and fourth generation of them that hate me".

We need to understand some things about idolatry and false images, for God is a jealous God. Ezekiel, chapter 8, speaks of the seat of jealousy when the prophet was lifted up. God is the only One who has the right to be jealous, and the seat of jealousy was in that holy place with the Lord. Whenever we become jealous, we take on an aspect of God that He has not given unto man, for man has no right to be jealous. He is a jealous God, and He doesn't want anything taking the glory from Him.

False images and idolatry exist when there is an excessive amount of love or admiration for a person or thing. Whenever a person is disappointed over something, it is possible that there is idolatry in this person's life. Even if we are looking to God as our source, if disappointment comes and we don't correct that thing quickly, it will produce bitterness. Every time an individual is bitter over a situation, it shows that they were in some form of idolatry...having certain expectations of that individual to give them something, which only God could grant. I don't care if it is personal. Only God can work through that person to do it. If they don't fulfill that, then we must trust that God will do it through someone else. Otherwise, we are moving in an areas of impatience.

God has stages of reproof. He will speak to us by the Holy Spirit to quicken something to us, or He will speak to us through other servants of God. He may speak to us through people around us who talk to us one on one, and they may say, "I don't even know why I am talking to you about this." But you know exactly what the Spirit of God is saying. Eventually, if we aren't obedient, God will turn us over to a reprobate mind, and He will allow an idol's voice to become clear to us.

In God's Word, we read where God sent a lying spirit into the mouths of the prophets, causing them to prophesy a lie. Sometimes we desire a thing so much that we actually move into an area of witchcraft.

I actually believe God will allow a lying spirit to come into mouths to confirm the voice of that idol that is in the heart of an individual so he can be turned over to his own judgment. This may be hard to chew, but let's look at Ezekiel 14.

> "Then came certain of the elders of Israel unto me, and sat before me.
> And the word of the Lord came unto me, saying, Son of man, these men have set up their idols in their heart, and put the stumbling block of their iniquity before their face: should I be inquired of at all by them?
> Therefore speak unto them, and say unto them, Thus saith the Lord God; Every man of the house

131

of Israel that setteth up his idols in his heart, and putteth the stumbling block of his iniquity before his face, and cometh to the prophet; I the Lord will answer him that cometh according to the multitude of his idols".

- Verses 1-4

Idolatry is totally subject. An idol can be anything. It can be something that we want so badly, we haven't even stopped to find out if it is the will of God. It can be a possession of some type, which we haven't even checked out with the Lord. We may have checked it out with Him and said, "I know God doesn't want me to have it. I'm just going to pray and believe God anyway." Sometimes God will allow things to come together supernaturally which aren't His will at all. Then, once we receive it, we say, "I wish I would have waited and obeyed God. The thing I desired so much I now have, but look what state I'm in."

The key in Verse 4 is, "...*I the Lord will answer him that cometh according to the multitude of his idols.*" Isn't it amazing that God will respond according to the multitude of the idols in our hearts? God goes through every available means to bring a person to repentance, to get him to change his heart, his mind, and his will about something. But if the person refuses and still wants to obey the thing that is an idol in his heart, worshipping that thing, believing that God will move through this thing rather than His

132

highest order, then the Lord will allow that thing to come to pass. He will speak through the multitude of the idols in your heart.

There was a time in Israel when God began to speak, and the people didn't want to believe the prophet Micaiah. They said, "He never has anything good to say." Eventually the Lord sent a lying spirit into the mouth of the prophets (I Kings 22). The lying prophets proclaimed, *"You will have victory."* They went up and met their destruction, because that was an idol in their hearts. We must be careful that our meditation does not cause us to bow to statues or idols, but we must bow down and submit our thought life, only, to that which is unctioned by the Holy Spirit. We get into vain imaginations when we meditate or constantly dwell on things that have no life in them. I have found that some believers desire a call of God or to be used of God in certain things so badly, but His grace is not upon them to function in that area. Because these people keep pressing, and pressing, and pressing, I have seen the Holy Spirit allow individuals to actually make a shipwreck of their lives, never fulfilling the real purpose for which God called them. God answered them through a multitude of idols, because of their own mindset and stubbornness.

God wants to teach us some things in this area. Anything can become an idol by taking preeminence in our lives. We need to monitor the things that become very important to us. Whenever a thing becomes outstanding in superiority, it will begin to speak in our lives. Anything that takes superiority and preeminence will overshadow the Voice of the Lord.

For example, let's consider a person who falls into fornication. The Spirit of God speaks to them. The first time they do it, God's voice of judgement is very loud. They are convicted. They say, "I really messed up. Lord, forgive me."

The second time they do it, they are convicted, but the conviction is not as strong. They say, "I messed up. Nobody is perfect, everybody else has failed. Look at the scandals that have occurred with the television ministers. I'm just a little weak in the flesh."

The third time it happens, they say, "I know I am with bad company. I know I need to do something about it, but God understands."

When you continue to sin, the voice of conviction becomes dimmer and dimmer. Eventually, as you continue in sin, there is no conviction at all. "Well, you know, in the sight of the Lord she and I are like one flesh anyway. God understands my heart, and He is faithful and just to forgive me of all sins." Eventually, the sin totally overshadows the Voice of the Lord. His Voice becomes faint, and the only voice left is that of the idol who will dictate, control, and maneuver your life.

I have seen people move completely out of God's

purposes because of an idol. One wrong move can throw your life into a dilemma and into a tailspin that you won't be able to reverse.

I have seen people relocate to another state because of an idol of the heart. "I must retire in Florida. Everyone is going to Florida. It is the place to be." They never asked God whether it was the place for them to be. Their lives were thrown into a dilemma, because they allowed that idol to speak in their lives much louder than the voice of the Lord.

We must insure that what we meditate upon is what God wants us to think on. What we meditate upon becomes the image of what we become.

The principle to remember is whatever we behold will be the thing that will speak to us. If we behold the Lord, that is Who we will hear. If we meditate upon a relationship, that is the voice we will hear. If we meditate upon our bills, that is what will speak to us.

Our checking account will speak to us. Have you ever heard the voice of your checkbook? You meditate upon that thing and it speaks loudly. If you don't know how to shake it off, it will convince you of all the "cannots," the "better nots," and impossibilities. Yet, God might be saying, "I want you to buy that house," and you say, "Yes, Lord, I know that You are speaking, but my checkbook has something to say." A lot of people reason themselves out of the purposes of God, because they allow an idol to take the preeminence. They allow a thing or circumstance to speak louder than the Voice of the Lord.

Whatever we meditate upon will be the thing that will speak in our lives!

The definition of a prophet [or seer] is "one who sees." Now, Jesus is our example of a seer.

"I speak that which I have seen with my Father: and ye do that which ye have seen with your father".

- John 8:38

Later, Jesus tells them who their father is. *"Ye are of your father the devil, and the lusts of your father ye will do..."* (Verse 44). Jesus is saying that we will do whatever we see our father do. If we are plagued by fear, that is what we will manifest. That is the thing that will speak loudly to us. That is the thing that will father us.

Jesus said, "I am doing what I see My Father do, and you are doing what you see your father do. You are out to kill Me, so we know who your father is. You have the life of your father in you."

That's why Jesus could look at Peter, and though he gave the mighty revelation that "Thou art the Christ, the Son of the Living God," that was something that came out of his spirit. But because his soul eclipsed his spirit, he tried to stop the Lord from moving into the Father's will. Jesus said to Peter, *"Get thee behind me, Satan,"* because Jesus recognized the spirit in which Peter was operating.

We must learn to discern in our thought life the things we need to denounce - those things that are eclipsing the Voice of the Lord.

> *"Then answered Jesus and said unto them, Verily, verily, I say unto you, The Son can do nothing of himself, but what he seeth the Father do: for what things soever he doeth, these also doeth the Son likewise".*

> - John 5:19

In this verse, we see a principle of the Kingdom, that we will only do that which we see the Father do. The Father wants us to discern what is in the cloud of covenant and what is in the glory cloud. We are to discern the Face and the Will of the Father in the cloud. It says, *"I will only do that which I see the Father do."*

We need to look within. Christ in us, the hope of glory. I will only do that which I see the Father do. Only then will we imitate the Lord and be followers of Jesus Christ.

The seer will become the vision which he beholds. Often, the prophet will act out the prophecy. They are able to become that which they behold. I know I'm on a fine edge, but do you know why it was not wrong for Hosea to marry a harlot? It would be wrong for you to marry a harlot, because you would be unequally yoked. Hosea and Gomer were an equal yoke in the mind of the Lord, because it was the will of the Father for Hosea to demonstrate something to Israel. Hosea's life became the Word of the Lord unto the people.

The seer must become that which he beholds the Father saying for him to become. That is why Jesus could whip the people out of the temple, and it would not be sin. Now, if you drive someone out of the temple, you will be in error, because that is not what the Father is showing you to do. Jesus whipped them and chased them out of the temple, because that was the will and the purpose of the Father. He was beholding the will of the Father.

The Word of God does not say, "My lambs know My Voice," but it says, "My sheep." That means grown up [mature]. It didn't say, "For as many as are led by the Spirit of God are the children of God," but they are the "sons" of God. The Greek word for son is HUIOS, which means "a fully matured son." When God speaks, I believe He reserves some things for the fully matured sons.

Galatians 4:1-2 says:

"Now I say, That the heir, as long as he is a child, differeth nothing from a servant, though he be lord of all;
But is under tutors and governors until the time appointed of the father".

Many of us, though we are children of God, are not yet sons of God, because God has us under tutors and governors.

Paul prayed:

"That the God of our Lord Jesus Christ, the Father of glory, may give unto you the spirit of wisdom and revelation in the knowledge of him:

The eyes of your understanding being enlightened; that ye may know what is the hope of his calling, and what the riches of the glory of his inheritance in the saints."

- Ephesians 1:17-18

The purpose for the eyes of our understanding to be opened is so we will receive the revelation of the Lord, which means a fuller knowledge of God.

Knowledge promotes growth in grace. II Peter 1:2, says that grace and peace are multiplied unto us through the knowledge of God and of Jesus, our Lord. As we receive more knowledge, we receive a greater measure of grace and peace.

The Spirit world must become more real to us than the natural world.

"For our light affliction, which is but for a moment, worketh for us a far more exceeding and eternal weight of glory;

While we look not at the things which are seen, but at the things which are not seen: for the things which are seen are temporal; but the things which are not seen are eternal".

- II Corinthians 4:17-18

139

God wants us to know that the things which are not seen are eternal.

II Corinthians 3:18 says, *"But we all, with open face beholding as in a glass the glory of the Lord, are changed into the same image from glory to glory, even as by the Spirit of the Lord."* We become whatever we worship. Whatever we behold in the glass, whatever we look at in imagery, whatever we behold in meditation, that is what we will become.

If we behold and have a fear of poverty, that image will hold us in bondage. If we bring poor people into a degree of prosperity, they often become some of the stingiest people on planet earth, because they still have a fear of being poor. They know what it is to suffer. They know what it is to endure lack. When God blesses them with things, they have a hard time releasing them, because they possess a fear of poverty.

When people are motivated through fear rather than faith, it is because of what they are beholding. We need to empty out our thought lives so we can behold some new images found in God's Word. Imagery of the Word can make the difference between a good preacher and a great preacher. It can also strengthen the degree and depth of the prophetic word. Often, people will have the right word, but they don't know how to place the image. If we know God wants to communicate an orange to someone, we must communicate that orange in such a way that they literally taste the orange in their mouths. If we sense that God is saying someone is to be free, we must find a way to communicate that.

There was a man who preached in such a way that the people actually felt the flames of hell when he was preaching. They felt as though they were in hell. Jesus wants to give us a way to communicate the Word of the Lord so people will see and then say, "Wow! That's it! That is so clear!"

The seer [or prophet] who has filled every corner of his mind with the pure Word of God, who has filled his heart with God's love, and who daily strives to "be like Jesus," will be able to communicate with a degree of clarity that the Body of Christ has not yet experienced.

The poor person who meditates upon God's Word shall prosper. The wounded person who meditates upon the Word of God shall be healed. Meditation is the key to reaching new horizons in God. Meditate, and eat the good of the land!!

The Role Of Meditation For The Prophet

VIDEO CASSETTES
BY BISHOP E. BERNARD JORDAN

RACIAL ETHICS OF THE KINGDOM
Confronts the intrinsic racism that has permeated Christian doctrine. A Thorough study of the "traditional" teachings of the Church unveils a deliberate strain of racism that fosters white supremacy and eradicates the image of God within the African-American. It was this same strain of religiosity that soothed the consciousness of many and justified the atrocities of slavery in America. This series delineates the patent effects of such doctrine and restores the dignity of all races under God that were created for His divine purpose. 4-Video series $80

FREEDOM: THE WAY OF LIBERATION
A clarification of God's true definition of freedom and the resulting implications of the facade of liberty that continues to enslave the African-American community. The continuous assault of malevolent imagery that society uses to deliberately cripple the function of an entire race of people and deface their cultural legacy actually recreates Jesus Christ, the anointed Deliver of men, into an effigy that is crucified afresh on a daily basis. True freedom will emerge as the traditions of men are dethroned and replaced by the uncompromising Word of God that will cut every insidious lie asunder. This series will offend many who have been blinded by the hypnotic lies that have lulled their purpose to sleep, and challenge others to look beyond the veil of mediocrity and prejudice and behold the beauty of God's original intention towards men. This four-tape series is an unforgettable encounter with past, present and future as it proclaims the manifest destiny of the African-American and the Kingdom of God. 4-Video series $80

A PASSAGE TO LIBERATION
"A Passage to Liberation" is a thought-provoking edict against the dichotomy of society's offer of "Liberation" towards the African-American, versus their true liberty as ordained by God. The ingrained levels of prejudice that are encountered on a daily basis are indicated through the ethical teachings of the Word of God. Your spirit will be stirred to defy the implied boundaries of racial denigration, and thrust into the zenith of your capabilities through Jesus Christ. 4-Video series $80

PREPARATION FOR LEADERSHIP
A scathing indictment upon the insidious racism that permeates American society. Using Exodus Chapter 2 as his premise, Bishop Jordan delivers a powerful comparison between the pattern of oppressive leadership that requires divine intervention in the affairs of men and culminated in the appointment of Moses as the deliverer of Israel with the oppressive leadership that the African-American encounters within society and within the walls of the Church. Frightening in its accuracy, this teaching, though disturbing to the ear, is truly the Word of the Lord for this hour, for there are serious ramifications that the Church must contend with if she is to bring a solution to the crisis of woe in this nation.
4-Video series $80

THE SPIRIT OF THE OPPRESSOR

This series, The Spirit of the Oppressor, by Bishop E. Bernard Jordan, attacks the very fiber of societal influence that manipulates the gospel to justify racial supremacy. The insidious attitudes that permeate the Church are also addressed, for judgment begins in the House of God. By understanding that the Church is called to be the example for the world to follow, this series is powerful in its ability to expose the evil that lurks in the shadows of the "acceptable norm," and echoes a clarion call for deliverance from the lie that masquerades as the truth. Are you REALLY ready for the Word of the Lord?

4-Video series .... $80 also available as a book.

NO MORE HANDOUTS

In this series, Bishop E. Bernard Jordan addresses an inflammatory issue that has been instilled as a mindset within an entire nation of people. The American society has methodically caused generations of African-Americans to become dependent to a system that keeps them in a cycle of expectation that the government will always be their source of blessing. Bishop Jordan delineates the intention of God to bring prosperity to His people, thus charging them to turn their attention from the governmental system and discover the treasure that God has placed in their hands, for God is to be their source! This series is challenging and will force you to use your God-given abilities to thing creatively and generate wealth. You don't need anyone's permission to increase, for God has already decreed that you would multiply and wax exceedingly mighty!! This radical message is for a radical people!! 4-Video series $80

THE CROSSING

Bishop E. Bernard Jordan delivers a powerful teaching that defines the attitude that one must take as they begin to cross over their Jordan into the promised land. The paradigms of the old must be shattered as the image of change comes into view. One cannot embrace a new day loaded with old apparatus that is inoperative; old concepts that only brought you to a place of desperation and frustration. Rather, one must search the Word of God and renew your mind to Kingdom thinking that will bring elevation into your life. This series will sweep the cobwebs of mediocrity out of your life, and provoke you to a higher plane of right thinking that will thrust you into the path of dreams fulfilled. Straightforward in his approach, Bishop Jordan preaches a message that is inflammatory to the lies that have taken residence in your mind, and instills the purity of truth that is the nature of Almighty God. 4-Video series $80

UNDRESSING THE LIE

In this series, Bishop E. Bernard Jordan addresses a crucial issue in the Body of Christ -- RACISM. This series will captivate those who are true lovers of truth, for Jesus Christ is the Truth, and many have hidden Him and His cultural reality from the eyes of many. By conducting a thorough search of the Scriptures, Bishop Jordan identifies the Bible's description of Jesus that has been marred by the lies of those who wished to destroy an entire nation's concept of themselves, instead rendering theology that warped the image of God and denigrated them by teaching that they were cursed. Questions that have wandering in the minds of many for hundreds of years are answered as Bishop Jordan takes a strong stand to unmask the lies that have been masquerading as Truth. 4-Video series $80

LEGACY

In this series, Bishop E. Bernard Jordan expounds upon the African presence within the Scriptures. Combatting the misnomers that Africans were cursed by God and that they had very little to do with the unfolding of Biblical events, Bishop Jordan smashes the veil of delusion to cause the obvious truth to surface. During this season, God is causing a cultural renaissance to emerge. The oppressor of American society has lulled the minds of most people into a stupor of ignorance leaving them landless, powerless, and, once again, easy to enslave. The historical accounts within the Scriptures have been bequeathed as a legacy from our ancestors to proclaim the Word of the Lord against the sophisticated genocide that is affecting the African-American. A nation that ignores its past is doomed to repeat its failures in the future. Bishop Jordan brings clarity and balance to an inflammatory topic that is frequently misunderstood. 4-Video series $80

ECONOMICS: THE PATH TO EMPOWERMENT

This vital tape series by Bishop E. Bernard Jordan and Prophet Robert Brown deals with God's answers to the financial instability that has crippled the strength of the African-American nation. By defining the true motivation behind the onslaught of racism, Bishop Jordan and Prophet Brown give clear answers to the persistent societal obstacles that prevent most people from obtaining the true manifestation of God's intention for prosperity in their lives. The articulate questions that proceed from the heart of the nation shall be answered through the accumulation of wealth, for money shall answer all things. This teaching will expose the subtle racism that affects your financial future, and will provoke you into a mindset that will see obstacles as opportunities so that the full potential of God within you may express in your success! 2-Video series $40

NO LIBERATION WITHOUT VIOLENCE

This series will cause one to Scripturally discern the validity of the message of liberation that echoed through America during the 60's through Dr. Martin Luther King and Malcolm X. By holding their messages up to the scrutiny of the Word of God, one cannot help but conclude whose message was more palatable to society, versus the message that stood in the integrity of the Scripture. Challenging in its content, this series is designed to attack the shackles of passivity and charge you to recognize the brutal realities of today's society. You are called to understand the true liberty of the gospel that Jesus preached. 4-Video series $80

A NEW GENERATION

Bishop E. Bernard Jordan is at his best in this series which portrays the change in one's attitude that must take place in order to attain your maximum potential in God and proceed to your Canaan Land! Like Joshua, one must be ready to be strong and of a good courage as you confront racism in this day. This is a radical message to eradicate error and bring forth the truth! Cutting in its intensity, this series will show you how the Word of the Lord will render you untouchable when you are aware of your purpose!! Bishop Jordan defines the new breed of people that God is raising up that will know the art of war, understand and love their enemy as they embrace the arms of destiny fulfilled.
4-Video series $80

BOOKS
BY BISHOP E. BERNARD JORDAN

THE MAKING OF THE DREAM

Are you riding the waves to an unknown shore? Is God's will passing you by? Is your God-given vision a dream or a reality? If you aren't sure of your life's destination then you need to hear "The Making of the Dream!" These teachings are remarkable because they will assist you in establishing workable goals in pursuit of success. You God-given dream will no longer be incomprehensible, but it will be touchable, believable and conceivable! $10

THE SCIENCE OF PROPHECY

A clear, concise and detailed exposition on the prophetic ministry and addresses many misnomers and misunderstandings concerning the ministry of the New Testament prophet. If you have any questions concerning prophetic ministry, or would like to receive sound, scriptural teachings on this subject, this book is for you! $10

MENTORING: THE MISSING LINK

Deals with the necessity of proper nurturing in the things of God by divinely appointed and anointed individuals placed in the lives of potential leaders. God's structure of authority and protocol for the purpose of the maturation of effective leadership is thoroughly discussed and explained. This book is highly recommended for anyone who believes that God has called them to any type of ministry in the Body of Christ. $10

MEDITATION: THE KEY TO NEW HORIZONS IN GOD

Designed to help you unlock the inner dimensions of Scripture in your pursuit of the knowledge of God. Long considered exclusively in the domain of New Age and eastern religions, meditation is actually part of the heritage of Christians, and is to be an essential part of every believer's life. We have been given a mandate to meditate upon the Word of God in order to effect prosperity and wholeness in our lives. This book gives some foundational principles to stimulate our transformation into the express image of Jesus Christ. $10

PROPHETIC GENESIS
Explores the realms of the genesis of prophecy...the beginning of God communicating to mankind. The prophetic ministry is examined in a greater depth, and the impact of various areas such as culture and music upon prophecy are taught in-depth. The prophetic ministry must always operate under proper authority, and this factor is also delved into. This book is designed for the mature student who is ready to enter into new dimensions of the prophetic realm. $10

THE JOSHUA GENERATION
A book that rings with the sound of confrontation, as the Body of Christ is urged to awaken from passivity to embrace the responsibility to fulfill the mandate of God in this hour! The Joshua Generation is targeted for those who are ready to look beyond the confines of tradition to tackle the weight of change. Are you a pioneer at heart? Then you are a part of The Joshua Generation!! This book is for you!! $10

SPIRITUAL PROTOCOL
Addresses an excruciating need for order and discipline in the Body of Christ. By aggressively attacking the trend of independence and lawless-ness that permeates the Church, the issue of governmental authority and accountability is thoroughly discussed. This manual clearly identifies the delineation of areas and levels of ministry, and brings a fresh understand-ing of authority and subsequent submission, and their implications for leadership within the House of the Lord. This is a comprehensive study that includes Bishop Jordan's earlier book, Mentoring, and is highly rec-ommended for anyone desiring to understand and align himself with God's order for the New Testament Church. $10

PRAISE AND WORSHIP
An extensive manual designed to give Scriptural foundation to the min-istry of the worshipping arts (musical, dramatic, artistic, literary, oratory, meditative and liturgical dance) in the House of the Lord. The arts are the outward mode of expression of an internal relationship with God, and are employed by God as an avenue through which He will speak and display His Word, and by man as a loving response to the touch of God upon his life. This book will compel the reader to deepen his rela-tionship with his Creator, and explore new degrees of intimacy with our Lord and Saviour, Jesus Christ. $20

BREAKING SOUL TIES AND GENERATIONAL CURSES

The sins of the father will often attempt to visit this present generation...however, those who understand their authority in Christ can refuse that visitation!! This series reveals the methods of identifying soul ties and curses that attempt to reduplicate themselves generation after generation. If you can point to a recurrent blight within your family lineage, such as premature death, familial diseases (alcoholism, diabetes, cancer, divorce, etc., then YOU NEED THIS SERIES!!!

Volume I .... 8-tape series.................$40.00
Volume II .... 8-tape series.................$40.00

WRITTEN JUDGMENTS VOLUME I

Chronicles the Word of the Lord concerning the nations of the world and the Body of Christ at large. Many subjects are addressed, such as the U.S. economy, the progress of the Church, the rise and fall of certain nations, and Bishop Jordan prophecies over every state in America with the exception of Ohio. This is not written for sensationalism, but to challenge the Body of Christ to begin to pray concerning the changes that are to come. $10

WRITTEN JUDGMENTS VOLUME II

A continuation of the Word of the Lord expressed towards the Middle East, the Caribbean nations, America, and the Body of Christ at large. Addresses various issues confronting America, such as abortion, racism, economics and homelessness. A powerful reflection of the judgements of God, which come to effect redemption and reconciliation in the lives of mankind. $10

MINI BOOKS

1. The Purpose of Tongues $1.00
2. Above All Things Get Wisdom...................$1.00
3. Calling Forth The Men of Valor...................$1.00

ORDER FORM

ZOE MINISTRIES
4702 FARRAGUT ROAD • BROOKLYN, NY 11203 • (718) 282-2014

TITLE	QTY	DONATION	TOTAL

Guarantee: You may return any defective item within 90 days for replacement. All offers are subject to change without notice. Please allow 4 weeks for delivery. No COD orders accepted. Make checks payable to ZOE MINISTRIES.

Subtotal _____

Shipping _____

Donation _____

TOTAL _____

Name: _____ Phone _____

Address: _____

_____Zip _____

Payment by: Check or Money Order (Payable to Zoe Ministries)
Visa • MasterCard • American Express • Discover

Card No.: _____ Exp. Date) _____

Signature (Required) _____

Appendix A
Physical Characteristics of
Some Radionuclides of
Interest in Nuclear Medicine

TABLE A–1. **Radiations Emitted in the Decay of ^{123}I ($\Gamma = 1 \cdot 53$ R·cm^2/ mCi·hr); T$_{\frac{1}{2}} = 13$ hr**

Number	Radiation (i)	Frequency of Emission (n_i)	Mean Energy (MeV) (E_i)
1	γ1	0.84	0.159
2	K Conversion Electron	0.13	0.127
3	L Conversion Electron	0.02	0.154
4	γ2	0.01	0.529
5	X-Ray-K (α)	0.71	0.027
6	X-Ray-K (β)	0.15	0.031
7	X-Ray-L	0.13	0.003
8	LMM Auger Electron	0.92	0.003
9	MXY Auger Electron	2.19	0.001

TABLE A–2. **Radiations Emitted in the Decay of ^{131}I ($\Gamma = 2 \cdot 2$ R·cm^2/ mCi·hr); T$_{\frac{1}{2}} = 8.1$ days**

Number	Radiation (i)	Frequency of Emission (n_i)	Mean Energy (MeV) (E_i)
1	β1	0.02	0.069
2	β2	0.07	0.096
3	β3	0.90	0.192
4	γ1	0.03	0.080
5	K Conversion Electron	0.03	0.046
6	γ2	0.06	0.284
7	γ3	0.82	0.364
8	K Conversion Electron	0.02	0.330
9	γ4	0.07	0.637
10	γ5	0.02	0.723

Data derived from Journal of Nuclear Medicine (Suppl. 10, 1975).

TABLE A–3. Radiations Emitted in the Decay of ^{201}Tl (Γ = 0.47 R · cm²/mCi · hr); T$_{1/2}$ = 73 hr

Number	Radiation (i)	Frequency of Emission (n_i)	Mean Energy (MeV) (E_i)
1	γ1	0.01	0.032
2	L Conversion Electron	0.21	0.018
3	M Conversion Electron	0.07	0.029
4	γ2	0.04	0.135
5	K Conversion Electron	0.10	0.052
6	L Conversion Electron	0.02	0.121
7	γ3	0.12	0.167
8	K Conversion Electron	0.18	0.084
9	L Conversion Electron	0.03	0.154
10	X-Ray-K (α)	0.78	0.070
11	X-Ray-K (β)	0.22	0.081
12	X-Ray-L	0.46	0.010
13	KLL Auger Electron	0.03	0.055
14	KLX Auger Electron	0.02	0.066
15	LMM Auger Electron	0.81	0.008
16	MXY Auger Electron	2.44	0.003

TABLE A–4. Radiations Emitted in the Decay of ^{133}Xe (Γ = 0·15 R·cm²/mCi·hr); T$_{1/2}$ = 5.3 days

Number	Radiation (i)	Frequency of Emission (n_i)	Mean Energy (MeV) (E_i)
1	β1	0.02	0.075
2	β2	0.98	0.101
3	γ1	0.01	0.080
4	K Conversion Electron	0.01	0.044
5	γ2	0.36	0.081
6	K Conversion Electron	0.53	0.045
7	L Conversion Electron	0.08	0.076
8	M Conversion Electron	0.03	0.080
9	X-Ray-K (α)	0.39	0.030
10	X-Ray-K (β)	0.09	0.035
11	X-Ray-L	0.08	0.004
12	Auger Electrons	1.67	0.003

TABLE A–5. Radiations Emitted in the Decay of ^{111}In (Γ = 1· R·cm²/mCi·hr); T$_{1/2}$ = 67.4 hr

Number	Radiation (i)	Frequency of Emission (n_i)	Mean Energy (E_i)
1	Gamma 1	0.90	0.17
2	K Conversion Electron	0.09	0.14
3	L Conversion Electron	0.01	0.16
4	Gamma 2	0.94	0.24
5	K Conversion Electron	0.05	0.22
6	L Conversion Electron	0.007	0.24
7	K (α) X-Ray	0.70	0.02
8	K (β) X-Ray	0.14	0.02
9	L-X-Ray	0.11	0.00
10	KLL Auger Electron	0.11	0.01
11	KLX Auger Electron	0.04	0.02
12	LMM Auger Electron	0.99	0.00

TABLE A–6. Radiations Emitted in the Decay of ^{67}Ga (Γ = 0· R·cm²/mCi·hr); T$_{1/2}$ = 78.1 hr

Number	Radiation (i)	Frequency of Emission (n_i)	Mean Energy (E_i)
1	Gamma 1	0.033	0.091
2	Gamma 2	0.38	0.093
3	K Conversion Electron	0.28	0.084
4	L Conversion Electron	0.038	0.092
5	M Conversion Electron	0.013	0.093
6	Gamma 3	0.24	0.185
7	Gamma 4	0.025	0.209
8	Gamma 5	0.16	0.300
9	Gamma 6	0.04	0.394
10	K-X-Ray	0.46	0.009
11	Auger Electron	0.66	0.008

Appendix B

CGS and SI Units

Quantity	CGS Units	MKS or SI Units	Conversion Factors* (CGS → MKS)
Length	Centimeter (cm)	Meter (m)	0.01
Mass	Gram (gm)	Kilogram (kg)	0.001
Time	Second (s)	Second (s)	1
Energy	erg	Joule (J)	10^{-7}
Radioactivity	Curie (Ci)	Becquerel (Bq)	3.7×10^{10}

Radiation
  Absorbed
  Dose
	rad	Gray (Gy)	0.01

Exposure	roentgen (R)	Coulomb/kilogram (C/kg)	2.58×10^{-4}
Dose Equivalent	rem	Sievert (Sv)	0.01

*To obtain results in the MKS system, multiply the CGS values by the conversion factor. To obtain results in the CGS system, divide the MKS values by the conversion factor.

Appendix C

Exponential Table

x	e^{-x}	x	e^{-x}	x	e^{-x}
0.00	1.00	0.22	0.80	0.60	0.55
0.01	0.99	0.24	0.79	0.65	0.52
0.02	0.98	0.26	0.77	0.693	0.50*
0.03	0.97	0.28	0.76	0.75	0.47
0.04	0.96	0.30	0.74	0.80	0.45
0.05	0.95	0.32	0.72	0.85	0.42
0.06	0.94	0.34	0.71	0.90	0.41
0.07	0.93	0.36	0.70	1.00	0.37
0.08	0.92	0.38	0.68	1.50	0.22
0.09	0.91	0.40	0.67	2.00	0.13
0.10	0.90	0.42	0.66	2.50	0.08
0.12	0.89	0.44	0.64	3.00	0.05
0.14	0.87	0.46	0.63	3.50	0.03
0.16	0.85	0.48	0.62	4.00	0.02
0.18	0.84	0.50	0.61	4.50	0.01
0.20	0.82	0.55	0.58	5.00	0.007

*See Chapter 3, p. 32

References and Suggestions for Further Reading

Chapters 1–4:
    Hendee, W.R.: *Medical Radiation Physics,* Second Ed., Chapters 1, 2 and 12. Year Book Medical Publishers, Inc., Chicago, 1979.
    Johns, H.E., and Cunningham, J.R.: *The Physics of Radiology,* Fourth Ed., Chapters 1 and 3. Charles C Thomas, Springfield, 1983.

Chapters 4 and 5:
    Radiopharmaceuticals, in *Seminars in Nuclear Medicine,* Vol. 4, No. 3, L.M. Freeman and M.D. Blaufox (Eds.). Grune and Stratton, Inc., New York, 1974.
    Radiopharmaceuticals, G. Subramanian, B.A. Rhodes, J.A. Cooper and V.J. Sodd (Eds.). The Society of Nuclear Medicine, Inc., New York, 1975.

Chapter 6
    Johns, H.E., and Cunningham, J.R.: *The Physics of Radiology,* Fourth Ed., Chapters 5 and 6. Charles C Thomas, Springfield, 1983.
    Rohrer, R.H.: The interaction of radiation with matter, in *Principles of Nuclear Medicine,* pp. 105–127. H.N. Wagner, Jr. (Ed.). W.B. Saunders Co., Philadelphia, 1968.

Chapter 7:
    Loevinger, R., and Berman, M.: A schema for absorbed dose calculations for biologically distributed radionuclides, *Journal of Nuclear Medicine,* Supplement No. 1, 1968.

Chapters 8 and 9:
    Cradduck, T.D.: Fundamentals of scintillation counting, in *Seminars in Nuclear Medicine,* 3:205–223, 1973.
    Instrumentation in Nuclear Medicine, Vol. 1, Chapters 4–6, 9, 10 and 12. G. Hine (Ed.). Academic Press, New York, 1967.

Chapters 10–13:
    Aronow, S.: Performance analysis of imaging systems, in *Seminars in Nuclear Medicine,* 3:239–257, 1973.
    Instrumentation in Nuclear Medicine, Vol. 1, Chapters 14, 16, 17 and 19. G. Hine (Ed.). Academic Press, New York, 1967.

Chapter 14:
    Craft, B.Y.: Single-Photon Emission Computed Tomography. Year Book Medical Pub-
        lishers, Inc. Chicago, 1986.
    Graham M.C., and Biegler R.E.: Principles of Positron Emission Tomography, in
        Physics of Nuclear Medicine, Recent Advances, Rao, Chandra & Graham (Eds.),
        American Association of Physicists in Medicine, 1984.

Chapter 15:
    The effect on populations of exposure to low levels of ionizing radiation, BEIR
        Report, Division of Medical Sciences. National Academy of Sciences. National
        Research Council, Washington, D.C., 1972.
    Pizzarello, D.J., and Witcofski, R.L.: Basic Radiation Biology, Second Ed. Lea &
        Febiger, Philadelphia, 1975.

Chapter 16:
    Shapiro, J.: Radiation Protection–A Guide for Scientists and Physicians. Harvard
        University Press, Cambridge, Mass., 1972.
    National Council on Radiation Protection (NCRP) Reports: 30, (1964); 37 (1970); 39
        (1971); 43, (1975); 48, (1976); 53 and 54, (1977).

General References for further reading
    Nuclear Medicine Physics, Instrumentation, and Agents, F.D. Rollo (Ed.), C.V. Mosby
        Co., St. Louis, 1977.
    Physics of Nuclear Medicine: Recent Advances, D.V. Rao, R. Chandra, and M.C.
        Graham (Eds), American Association of Physicists in Medicine, 1984.

Index

Page numbers in italics refer to illustrations;
page numbers followed by a t refer to tables.